PE—To the parishioners of St. Matthew's Episcopal Church, Maple Glen, PA and St. Thomas's Episcopal Church, Whitemarsh, PA. And, as always, to my family.

JB—To Dave Detwiler, who constantly reminds me that the Church is full of "normal people."

Contents

Infomercial

This book is a brief guide to reading the book of Genesis. This book is not for scholars or seminary students, but we will gladly sell them a copy if they want one. We wrote this for normal people like you—people who are curious about the Bible and want to get a handle on what Genesis is about; people who don't want to spend the next five years of their lives learning Hebrew or slogging through thousands of pages of details. We know how it is. You want to get to the point. And we want to help.

Some of you might be curious about how to read Genesis because of certain controversies you have heard about, like the relationship between evolution and Genesis. Well, calling it a "relationship" might be a stretch. We'll just say that science and Genesis have not been the best of friends over the last few hundred years. They do, after all, tell very different stories about how the earth and life on earth began. And the more science does its work, the harder it is to make sense of Genesis, which can start to make you nervous if you take the Bible seriously.

Though this book is not about that relationship, it might help move it along. Why? Because one of the bigger problems in the debate over Genesis and science is that people, on both sides of the controversy, think they can just compare the days of creation (Genesis 1) or the story of Adam and Eve (Genesis 2–3) to the theory of evolution and somehow find answers to what happened at the beginning.

But you can't do that. These two stories in Genesis are actually *small* parts of a much *larger* story: the whole book of Genesis. And the focus of Genesis is not on creation but on the nation of Israel. And Genesis itself is a small part of an even larger story: the Pentateuch (the first five books of the Bible), which is of course a small part of the entire Old Testament. So, even though this book is not about science and the Bible, it will help those concerned or curious about those debates by taking a look at the whole story of Genesis and finding out what we should expect from its first chapters.

Whether or not you have an interest in the controversies about Genesis and science, you've still come to the right place to learn about Genesis. We wrote this book to help normal people get a feel for what the story of Genesis, as a whole, is about. We want to help you see Genesis as one story, not just a bunch of small (and weird) stories that stand on their own—which is how most people learn to read Genesis from childhood. Nothing in Genesis stands on its own. All the stories are connected and they all serve a purpose in the whole.

And part of the task of reading Genesis as a story is to learn to read Genesis through ancient eyes, rather than modern ones. The big question in front of us is why Genesis looks the way it does. Of all the stories the Israelites could tell, and in all the ways they could have told them, why *this* way?

As we will see, one primary answer to this question is seen in the image that opens the second chapter, the nineteenth-century painting "Jacob Wrestling with the Angel." That painting illustrates the famous wrestling match in the heart of Genesis, between Jacob and a divine being of some sort. After the match, Jacob is given a new name, "Israel," which means "struggling with God." We will find several major themes as we make our way, but a key idea that you will see throughout is how much God's chosen people struggle with God. Keeping this in front of you as you read Genesis will help some of the pieces come together.

Finally, one last disclaimer. We couldn't get to everything. If we tried to include all the details in Genesis and all the things that have been said about them, you would have to upgrade your e-reader. We didn't want to write *War and Peace: Genesis Edition*, and you wouldn't want to read it. But our hope is that once you get the big picture, you can finally tackle Genesis on your own, spending the rest of your life getting all the details.

Rembrandt's "Jeremiah Lamenting Over the Destruction of Jerusalem," 17th century Public Domain

1

The Genesis of Genesis

Genesis Is a Story

Genesis is an ancient story. This may sound like an obvious or even patronizing way to begin. Of course it's an ancient story. But once we look at what this means, that short phrase might be the most important thing to remember about Genesis. It will guide the rest of this book, showing us how to approach Genesis and what we should expect from it.

Depending on our past exposure to the Bible, some of us might approach Genesis expecting to find a detailed account of history as though it's a modern textbook. Of course, by calling Genesis a story, we are not saying anything about whether it is historical or fictional. Any book about the American Revolution or the Cuban Missile Crisis is just as much a story as Herman Melville's classic *Moby Dick* or even the sitcom "Modern Family." But Genesis is not a textbook—history, science, or otherwise. Let the teenager in us rejoice.

Instead of a textbook, some of us might approach Genesis as a book of principles to teach us how to live. But if we approach a story like a book of principles, it is likely we will find ourselves wanting to know what every passage "means for me." Imagine trying to watch a riveting blockbuster or a moving drama while pausing it every five minutes to ponder how that scene might apply to your life. Stories do apply to our lives, perhaps more than any other form of literature, but not as abstract principles or proverbs. They apply when our personal story collides with them, when we get lost in the world they present to us.

So when we read Genesis as an ancient story, written at a particular time to a particular people, it opens up possibilities and worlds we don't encounter in our limited existence. When we stop using Genesis as an argument, a textbook, or a code of conduct, and begin to see it as an ancient story—with memorable characters, twists and turns, ups and downs, accomplishments and mistakes—we find it fresh, deep, and more true and relevant than we might expect.

The best stories shape our lives precisely because as we read them, we are presented with both reality and possibility. The characters and circumstances resonate with us because they are mirrors of our own story, reminding us that we are not alone in our experiences. But they also pull us toward another world that we are less familiar with, a world that is often strange and sometimes dangerous, a world that doesn't show me what is, but what is possible.

Why would we expect anything less at the beginning of the story of God's relationship with humanity? But in order to see Genesis through ancient eyes, we have to admit that our modern eyes might get in the way. So this chapter is eye surgery. It is meant to help us suspend our twenty-first-century gaze and allow us to enter a new way of looking at the world.

Genesis Is Book One in a Series

Imagine if someone said to you they understood your favorite epic saga, perhaps *Star Wars, The Lord of the Rings*, or *Harry Potter*. But you come to find out they had only read the first book in the series. How much of the story could they possibly have understood? Doesn't the beginning of a story really only make sense in light of the middle and the end? In the same way, if you want to get a handle on Genesis (and you do, which is why you bought this book), you really have to take a step back and recognize that Genesis is the first book of a five-part series.

The shorthand title for this series among scholars is the Pentateuch (from the Greek, meaning "five scrolls") and it contains the first five books of the Bible: Genesis, Exodus, Leviticus, Numbers, and Deuteronomy. So Genesis is the *Fellowship of the Ring / Philosopher's Stone / Hunger Games / Twilight* (did we miss anyone?) of the Pentateuch. And since Genesis is the first book in a series, we will miss a lot if we don't take time to understand the entire story of the Pentateuch first before turning to Genesis.

The Pentateuch is very old—far older than Christianity. It comes to us from the ancient Israelites who call these first five books the *Torah*, from the Hebrew for "law" or "instruction." And it's useful for us to understand why the ancient Israelites call this five-part story the *Torah*. Just like the title to most movies and books, it gives us a hint as to what the story is about. And much to your surprise, it's not called *Torah* because it's a list of tedious *thou shalts* and *thou shalt nots* to skip over. Don't get us wrong. There are laws dispersed here and there throughout the story that are tedious—even weird and awkward—for modern readers (concerning mildew, wet dreams, eating pork or camel meat, what kind of bird to sacrifice, what happens if your bull gores a neighbor, etc., etc., snooze). If you read the Pentateuch, you'll have to take all that in stride (or just keep doing what you've been doing and skip those parts).

Jews call these five books *Torah* because the climactic moment of the entire story is when a specific God, named Yahweh, meets with Israel on Mt. Sinai and gives Israel the instructions for how to be his people (after they are delivered from Egypt in the book of Exodus). The Israelites are camped out at Mt. Sinai for a little more than half of the Pentateuch. Clearly, this period is the "center" of the story, the event that everything before is leading up to and everything after is reflecting on.

Mt. Sinai is where the Israelites receive God's law (hence the name *Torah*) and this law is central to their identity as God's people. It reveals their relationship to God as his people and their relationship to the land as God's gift. In other words, the story of Israel finds its climax at Sinai because there they find out (1) who they are as God's people, and (2) how to maintain a life-giving relationship with God in the Promised Land.

So if we are going to read Genesis as the ancient Israelites would have, we have to read it as a story that propels us to the dramatic and climactic events of Mt. Sinai. We shouldn't be surprised to find in Genesis some of the same themes we find at Sinai. Again and again in Genesis, we will find hints of where the story is headed.

If the events at Mt. Sinai are the "climax" of the Pentateuch, the "message" of the Pentateuch is this:

> Listen up, Israel. Yahweh is the creator of the cosmos. He also redeemed you from Egypt and gave you the land of Canaan as a home. You are his people and he alone is your God, worthy of your complete devotion.

That's what the story of the Pentateuch is getting at and why the events at Sinai are so central. Through the stories it tells, Israel is reminded, even admonished, that Yahweh, and not any other god, is to be worshipped. Worshipping other gods in the ancient world—with every house, village, and nation having its own list of favorite gods—was as easy as deciding between restaurants today. But, in the midst of all this choice between gods, the Pentateuch reminds the Israelites that they are to remain loyal to one God, that Yahweh alone is worthy of worship. Why?

> Because this God alone is (1) the creator of the world and (2) the savior of Israel.

Okay, so where does Genesis come in? Genesis sets the stage by focusing on (1) and hinting at (2). The rest of the Pentateuch focuses on (2) (the exodus from Egypt) while reminding us of (1). And once you get outside of the Pentateuch, much of the Old Testament still centers on these two themes—usually by showing how Israel tends to forget that the creator is also their redeemer. Genesis introduces us to God as the creator and gives us flash previews of God as savior. Actually, we'll see that creating and redeeming are two sides of the same coin.

To sum up, we are saying that Genesis has to be read as a *story* to be understood properly. But the story we find in Genesis was written in a world that looked very different than ours. If we are to read it well, we must also read it through *ancient* eyes.

Genesis Is Ancient

It's easier to understand what you are reading if you know *when* it was written and under what *circumstances*. Orwell's *Animal Farm* might make sense as a cute (better, disturbing) story about talking animals. But knowing *when* it was written (1945) and the *circumstances* that led to it being written (a critique of Joseph Stalin's oppressive Communist regime) will help you see that the book is actually an allegory. If you don't catch that, you miss the whole point. In other words, knowing at least something about the *historical* context of a story—when a story was written and under what circumstances—makes you a better reader.

The same is true of Genesis.

Just because Genesis is in the Bible doesn't mean we can

read it any way we please. And it certainly doesn't mean that the stories were written with twenty-first century readers in mind. Whether we say that Genesis was written by ancient Israelites or even by God *to* ancient Israelites doesn't change the fact that Genesis was written a long, long time ago, in a language that is now essentially dead (Jews in Israel today speak a different form of Hebrew). Genesis is really old, and if we are going to read it well, we have to make adjustments in our thinking.

How Ancient Is Genesis?

So, when, exactly, in the ancient world was Genesis written? What was happening in the life of the Israelites or in the world around them? Here we run into our first problem with Genesis, and most any other piece of ancient literature: Genesis is an anonymous book.

Genesis has no title page, no author's name, no date of publication stamped into it, no dedication page. Jewish and Christian traditions have generally labeled Moses as the author of the Pentateuch—after all, he is the main character. But there are a few very good reasons why that label won't stick, and biblical scholars (and a few Jews and Christians long before that) have been talking about them for the past 300 years.

For one thing, it would be slightly creepy for Moses to have written the Pentateuch since it records his death and burial (Deuteronomy 34). The writer even tells us that "to this day" no one knows where Moses is buried (34:7), and that since Moses' day no one has ever arisen like him (34:10–12). That sounds like it was written a long, long time after Moses' death, thinking back to the good old days.

Actually, the whole Pentateuch reads like a story about the distant past, with Moses and other characters spoken of in the third person. The Pentateuch is a story *about* Adam, Noah, Abraham, Isaac, Jacob, Joseph, and *about* Moses and the Israelites who left Egypt and went to Mt. Sinai. It's a bit odd to think of Moses talking about himself in the third person—only

NBA players do that. Plus, in one place in the Pentateuch, we read that Moses was more humble than anyone on earth (Numbers 12:3). Would a truly humble man write about himself this way? It makes more sense to say someone else at a later time described Moses this way.

There are other reasons that clue us in that someone other than Moses wrote the Pentateuch, but we don't need to take time for that here. But if you are dying to know, check out the other books we recommend in the "Further Reading" section at the end of this book. The real question is, Who did write it and when did he live?

To answer that question, scholars have had to engage in some historical detective work. And their detective skills have led them to agree that the Pentateuch *as we know it* didn't come together until sometime after 539 B.C. (about 700–1000 years after the period of Moses). This is a significant year for Jews. The year 539 B.C. is when the Persian King Cyrus defeated the Babylonians, thus releasing the Israelites who had been captives of Babylon since 586 B.C.

When we say the Pentateuch "as we know it" came together sometime after 539 B.C., we do not mean to say it was written from scratch during that time. There were certainly older writings and oral traditions that had been around for hundreds of years. But it was sometime after the Israelites returned to their homeland that all of these older writings and oral traditions were compiled and edited in the way we now have them in our Bible. So rather than viewing the Pentateuch as a song written by one artist at one time, it should be seen as a remix that takes samples of other work and puts them together in a fresh way to tell a single story. This goes for Genesis, too.

Why would anyone come to this conclusion? Because there are clues in Genesis that point you in this direction, some of which have been noted by Jewish and Christian readers for hundreds of years.

For example, in the Abraham story (Genesis 12:6 and 13:7) we read that the Canaanites were living in the land "then" or "at that time." If the Canaanites were living in the land "then," it makes sense that the writer is writing at a time when the Canaanites were *not* in the land. And according to the biblical story, it wasn't until the days of Kings David and Solomon that the Canaanites were driven out, which was sometime after 1000 B.C. So here we have a clue that at least that part of Genesis comes from sometime after 1000 B.C., though it is telling us a story set in Abraham's day (about 2100 B.C., as the Bible presents it).

Another example is Genesis 36, where we read a list of the kings of Edom. The writer introduces the list this way: "These are the kings who reigned in the land of Edom, before *any king reigned over the Israelites.*" The writer says "before any king reigned" because he lived during or after the time when Israel did have kings, which, again, did not happen until about 1000 B.C.

For these reasons and more, scholars feel that Israel's story began to be written down around the time of King David. That's when the Israelites were pretty settled in the land of Canaan and had some peace and quiet to think things through. And now that they were a nation, they certainly began to keep records (which were the foundation for books like 1 and 2 Samuel and 1 and 2 Kings) and write down their songs for worship (Psalms). They probably also began writing down their own ancient oral stories, recording their traditions from hundreds and hundreds of years back.

Israel's National Catastrophe

Writing Israel's story probably started around the time of King David, but it went into hyperspeed when the Israelites went through the trauma of the exile as they were taken out of their country and into Babylon in the sixth century B.C. Why would that make them write more? The Israelites believed God had promised, ages earlier, to give them the land of Canaan to be theirs forever. He also promised that they would have a line of kings descended from King David who would reign from

Jerusalem forever. (You can read about this in 2 Samuel 7.) But Israel (especially the kings) had blown God off for so long that, as the story goes, God gave them over to their enemies, the Babylonians—who had recently become the superpower.

The Babylonians marched into Jerusalem and by 586 B.C. had bulldozed the Temple, God's sacred house, and taken much of the population captive. So in 586 B.C. Israel looked around. No king. No land. No Temple. Who is Israel without a king, without a land, and without the Temple? It looked like God had broken his promise and abandoned his own people.

It's not hard to imagine, then, why the Israelites at this time did some soul searching. They looked back at their ancient past to make sense of the tragedy of their recent history. "In view of all that happened, are we still God's people? Does he still care for us? How can we make sure that this doesn't happen to us again? Will we ever regain the glory of our past?" To address these very real and pressing questions, they began retelling their story—one last time. That last telling became what Christians call the Old Testament.

> Think of the Old Testament as Israel's story, written in light of national trauma, to encourage continued faithfulness to God.

The Pentateuch recounts how the Israelites got their start and how God stuck by them, and gave them the gift of law and tabernacle on Mt. Sinai. It also reminds them of how they got into this mess: their failure to be faithful to God, who was faithful to them. Renewing their commitment to their faithful God was the front-burner issue now that they were back home after the exile. The Pentateuch encouraged them that God's faithfulness can always be counted on no matter what.

The Pentateuch is Israel's constitution: "This is who we are, this is where we have come from, this is what we believe—and most importantly, this is what our God is like. He has always been faithful to us in the past, no matter how badly we screwed up. But he also commands us to be faithful. Let's make sure we remember all this so we aren't carried off by another nation ever again." The Israelites were humiliated and held captive by the Babylonians for about fifty years. Throw into the mix the fact that a generation or two was born in Babylon during the exile, meaning they likely had no connection to the past. When you put it that way, a book that ties together past and present sounds like a great idea.

Think of Eastern European immigrants to America talking about "the old country," and within a generation their children are getting Metallica tattoos and body piercings. The possibility of caving in to Babylonian customs—and Babylonian gods—was a constant pressure. So, it's not surprising that some stories in Genesis seem to be explicitly anti-Babylon. We'll see examples as we go.

So how we read Genesis depends on us knowing these circumstances, just like knowing about Stalin is vital for us to understand *Animal Farm*. Knowing that Genesis as we have it in our Bibles is written as a part of the Pentateuch, and that the Pentateuch is written as Israel's constitution in light of the traumatic events of the Babylonian exile helps us read this story with ancient eyes.

As an analogy, think of the American Declaration of Independence. This document established America's national identity and was written at a time of crisis, to *oppose* their British "oppressors" (with all due apologies to our British friends). If you didn't know that background, it would be difficult to understand why the Declaration of Independence sounds like it does. Imagine an archaeologist unearthing the Declaration of Independence 5,000 years from now, without knowing anything about America and its fight for independence. Without a working knowledge of what the colonists were opposing, the words of their Declaration lose a lot of their force. In the same way, when we see that the Pentateuch, Israel's "Constitution," is partly written as a theological response to Babylonian captivity, some important pieces fall into place.

We have spent this chapter saying something rather simple: you cannot properly understand Genesis without seeing it first in *its* context, not ours. Genesis not only begins the story of Israel and should be read in conversation with the rest of that story, but it is also a story that is told through the eyes of an ancient people in national crisis. The Bible truly has a story to tell and a point to make, and it all begins in the beginning. Keeping both of these points in mind, let's turn to the first book of our Bible, Genesis.

Leloir's "Jacob Wrestling with the Angel,"
19th century Public Domain

2

Genesis from 30,000 Feet

Now that we have established that Genesis is an ancient story, let's take a little tour of where we are headed. The book of Genesis is fifty chapters long. It takes us from Adam to Joseph, from the creation of the cosmos to Israel's entrance into Egypt. These fifty chapters of Genesis are usually divided into two main parts, Genesis 1–11 and Genesis 12–50.

But before we go any further, we have a confession to make. If we were truly reading Genesis through ancient eyes, we would have to get rid of "chapters" altogether. The ancient Israelites didn't have chapters or verse numbers. Christian monks added them centuries later to help readers find their way through the Bible. (And we are most grateful to these blessed monks. Imagine trying to find a passage without chapter and verse numbers.) But the Bible did not start out that way.

Instead of chapters, Genesis introduces new sections with

the phrase, "This is the account of." This phrase shows up ten different times. Six are found in chapters 1–11 and the other four in chapters 12–50.

> Genesis 2:4: "This is the account of the heavens and the earth."
> Genesis 5:1: Line of Adam.
> Genesis 6:9: Line of Noah.
> Genesis 10:1: Line of Noah's sons.
> Genesis 11:10: Line of Shem (one of Noah's sons).
> Genesis 11:27: Line of Terah (Abraham's father).
> Genesis 25:12: Line of Ishmael (Abraham's son by the slave girl Hagar).
> Genesis 25:19: Line of Isaac (Abraham's son by his wife Sarah).
> Genesis 36:1: Line of Esau (Isaac's elder son).
> Genesis 37:2: Line of Jacob (Isaac's younger son, renamed Israel).

These ten sections make a lot of sense if we remember that Genesis is the beginning of *Israel's* story. Genesis moves us toward Jacob, who will be renamed Israel, and his sons will the patriarchs of the twelve tribes of Israel.

If we are going to read Genesis with ancient eyes, we'll need to keep these ten "accounts" in mind as we move through the "fifty chapters" we are familiar with. In fact, the chapter and verse divisions the monks gave sometimes interrupt the flow of the story, making us think there is a break when there isn't (what were those monks thinking?). So even though we will stick with the traditional fifty chapters you have come to know and love (and rely on) so that we can keep things simple, we want you to keep in mind that these "accounts" are better guides to the stories we find in Genesis and how they all hang together. They help us remember where the story is heading.

Genesis in 554 Words

Part one of Genesis, chapters 1–11, tells the story of the creation of the cosmos, Adam and Eve, the slaying of their son Abel by his older brother Cain, Noah's ark, and the tower of Babel. In between are interspersed a family tree and a list of nations after the flood.

These eleven chapters are more familiar—and more controversial—than any others in Genesis. They are also the most misunderstood, which is a big fat shame. Just like the first chapters of your favorite novel, this section sets up some key themes that will show up throughout Genesis as well as the rest of the Pentateuch. Asking the wrong questions here will lead to major confusion later.

Chapters 1–11 set us up for the second part of Genesis, chapters 12–50. Have you ever noticed that movies often have a dramatic opening sequence to capture your attention and to give you some background on what's about to happen? One of the best at this is the movie *Up*. The opening sequence sets up the entire background for the story in about a minute. Brilliant. Then roll title and credits, followed by the start of the main narrative.

Genesis 1–11 is the opening sequence that grabs your attention and provides the setting for Genesis 12–50, the story of Israel from Abraham to Egypt, from one man to a people, or more specifically, a large clan. (They won't become a full-fledged nation or kingdom until after Israel leaves Egypt and sets up shop in Canaan many centuries later.) But every nation has humble beginnings, and Israel's begins in Genesis 12–50. There, we see how a Mesopotamian man (from Babylon, no less) named Abraham was chosen by God (without explanation) to leave his homeland and travel to Canaan with his wife Sarah.

Abraham was called by God and promised two things: people and land. Genesis 12–50 is a story of Israel's ups and downs and how that roller coaster soap opera will pan out. Where is this dual promise of offspring and land going? Will God come through if Israel keeps behaving badly? Will the pattern of stubbornness and disobedience of chapters 1–11 keep repeating itself? How is God going to handle all this?

After we follow the story through Abraham and Isaac, we are introduced to Jacob, Abraham's grandson. Here, amid stories of deceit, plots to murder, and searching for a wife, we find that the promise is alive in this unlikely son, Jacob. God changes Jacob's name to Israel, which brings the story of Genesis into focus. Israel's twelve sons are ancestors of the twelve tribes of Israel, the nation that will be center stage for the rest of the Old Testament.

The last third of Genesis turns our attention to one of those sons, Joseph. Thrown into a well by his brothers, he winds up in Egypt with near-supreme power. After some on-the-edge-of-your-seat family drama (that Dreamworks happily cashed in on), Genesis ends with Jacob's death and all twelve sons and their families in Egypt. Of course, this is the perfect setup for the sequel, which we find in the famous story of the Exodus (another story Dreamworks happily cashed in on, though we still prefer our Moses looking like Charlton Heston instead of one of the Backstreet Boys).

A Self-Centered Story

And that is the CliffsNotes version of Genesis that will hopefully help you as we get further and further into the details of the story. But before we do, we want to point out a few landmarks that will help to remind you that you're on the right path. If this really is a story about Israel, edited by Israelites returned from exile and wondering about their relationship to God, we should expect to see that in the story. And we do.

Genesis is all about Israel as recipient of God's promise of people and land. Keep your eyes open as you try to read as an ancient Israelite and you might find yourself surprised at how often the themes of land and people show up. Actually, you will see the *struggle* between Israel and God over land and people.

We find ourselves reading about some struggle at every

point in the story: creation (we'll explain next chapter), Adam, Cain, Noah, and Abraham and his offspring. Siblings especially seem to struggle a lot. And if you need more convincing that struggling is a big issue in Genesis, look at Jacob. He literally wrestles with God and his new name, "Israel," means "one who struggles with God." This is exactly what we would expect from a story written by exiled Israelites who are struggling with their current conditions, and ultimately, their very identity.

And lastly, we should find evidence that these stories are trying to connect an exiled audience with their ancient past. These Israelites were not interested in reading about Noah because it's a great story or because it has a great principle to live by. And they weren't interested in trying to find out "what really happened" as a modern historian might. They were writing and reading these stories to understand their own relationship with God. So we will find several places where these stories tell us a lot about how later Israelites saw themselves and how it is reflected in the stories we find in Genesis.

God's relationship with Israel. People. Land. Struggle. This is the story of Genesis.

"God the Geometer,"
mid-13th century Public Domain

3

Genesis 1: Yahweh Is Better

When we read through ancient eyes, the beginning of Genesis is actually quite dramatic. Ironically, we might be too familiar with this story to see it that way. Christians are trained to think that Genesis begins this way: God made a ball of cosmic Play-Doh appear of out nowhere.

But that doesn't sound like what's happening here in Genesis 1 and it doesn't sound like the type of story the ancient Israelites would tell about how their God creates. Now, it's true that some New Testament passages, like Colossians 1:16 and Hebrews 11:3 (perhaps under the influence of Greek ways of thinking) mention God creating something out of nothing. But when you have a minute, look at 2 Peter 3:5, which talks about creation in more of an ancient Israelite way: "the earth was formed out of water and by means of water."

So, right here, in the first two verses of Genesis, we have to work hard to leave the modern world behind to figure out exactly what is happening.

> In the beginning, when God began to create the heavens and the earth, the *earth was chaotic* and darkness covered *the face of the deep*, while a wind from God swept over *the face of the waters.*

Despite the words, "In the beginning," it feels like we are walking in on the middle of something. And that's because we are. We begin with an earth that is an empty and mysterious "deep," which we find out is the same thing as the "waters" at the end of the passage. Confused?

Now you can see why we spent so much time reminding you that this is an *ancient story* by the *Israelites*, or an *ancient story* by God *to* the *Israelites*. If it is written by and to the Israelites, we need to see it from their point of view. If we are going to understand this story we have to suspend our twenty-first-century views of the universe, science, and history, and enter their world. If their world seems strange to you, just try it on and wear it for a few minutes, even if it makes you feel a little insecure. Because what we find is that this new, strange, way of seeing the opening of Genesis would make perfect sense in the ancient world.

Chaos Has a Rough Week

Other stories of creation in the ancient world never start with nothing and go to something. In fact, these stories simply aren't interested in how the universe got here, at least not in any scientific sense. Actually, they weren't thinking of a "universe" at all, but the *cosmos*, as we shall see in a moment. We might be tempted to ask, "Where did this desolate earth and deep waters come from, if God didn't create them out of nothing?" The answer from Genesis 1: silence interrupted by chirping crickets.

We aren't told. Get used to it—we'll get that answer a lot. Instead, this story focuses on the earth being "chaotic" or, as some translations say, a "formless void," and water seems to have something to do with why.

The Hebrew phrase for "formless void" is *tohubohu*, which is not a new elitist foodie food group, but two Hebrew words that have been combined to make a word that has actually made it into English (we're not kidding, look it up). *Tohu* means formless and *bohu* means empty. In English, the phrase has come to mean something utterly *chaotic*. And when we use the word "chaos" (instead of "nothing") for what we find at the beginning of Genesis, we are beginning to understand the ancient mindset about how God creates.

In the ancient world of biblical times, the gods did not "create out of nothing." The world looks the way it does because the gods "tamed the chaos." Genesis is Israel's story about who is truly responsible. The uniqueness of Israel's God in an ancient mindset is not that he creates out of nothing, but the swift, invincible power he displays in overcoming chaos, working solo in the span of a work week. Israel's story stands in stark contrast to the stories of Israel's neighbors, as we will see in a moment.

So, how does God tame the chaos? First, where there is no "form" (*tohu*) God will make habitable, ordered space. Then, where there is emptiness (*bohu*) God will fill it. Days 1–3 *create space* and Days 4–6 *fill the space*. The whole chapter is structured as an answer to the "formless void" problem we see in verses 1–2. When we see the opening scene of Genesis in this way, we find the six days of creation making even more sense. They aren't trying to tell us how the universe was created out of nothing or allegorically telling us how God used evolution. Instead, these days display for us the creative act of Israel's God, a very purposeful ordering of the chaos into a place of order.

Imagine that it's game night at your house and your family wants to play Monopoly. But, much to your chagrin, the kitchen table is stacked with junk mail, backpacks, old snacks, grocery lists, and some sticky stuff left over from breakfast. You can't play the game until you make room for the board, the stacks of money, and a place for you all to sit. So, you start to work systematically clearing out the mess so you can get ready to play. You're not playing yet. You just created the space. After you have done all of this preparation, you are ready to put things in their place—board goes here, money goes there, pieces go here, some room for snacks and drink, and you all take your proper place around the table so you can begin playing.

This is similar to what is happening in Genesis 1: you have to put things in order (Days 1–3) before you can start setting up the game and start playing (Days 4–6). We begin Genesis with a cluttered kitchen table—a dark, churning ocean and nothing else. The deep. And we ask ourselves: "How in the world is God going to create the beauty we see in the world today out of *this* mess?" And just like family game night, Days 1–3 of creation "order the chaos" by creating space for something new. And then Days 4–6 "put down the pieces" in this newly created space.

On Day 1, God "creates a space" for the sun, moon, and stars by separating the light from the dark. Notice, he doesn't create the sun, moon, and stars (the things that actually give us light) until Day 4. (Actually, the moon *reflects* light, but the Israelites didn't know that.) On Day 1, he is "clearing off the table" so that there is room for the sun, moon, and stars on Day 4. That is, he is "creating order out of chaos" so that in Day 4, he can fill this newly created "space" with the sun, moon, and stars.

On Day 2, God creates a space for birds and sea creatures (basically things that don't need dry land in the ancient mind) by separating the "waters above from the water below" with what is called a "firmament," or in some translations, an "expanse." We will see in a moment how we should think of this firmament. But for now, the important thing is that he does this so that on Day 5 he can fill this newly created "space" with sea creatures and birds. Then on Day 3, he moves the oceans to the side to allow dry land to appear so that on Day 6 he can create land animals and finally humans. So on Days 1–3 God "clears off the table," and on Days 4–6 he "sets up the game."

That is the overall picture painted for us in Genesis 1. We begin with chaos, with *tohubohu*, and by the time we get to the end of the chapter, we have air, land, and sea, and all those things that fill those spaces. Chaos is ordered and the cosmos is filled. God has done his work, with little effort, in six days.

Now that we have the big picture down, there are a few details that the storyteller wants his readers to see.

A Reminder to Israel and a Slap in the Face to Everyone Else (Especially the Babylonians)

Remember in the first chapter when we mentioned that Genesis sometimes has a Babylonian "feel" to it? If Genesis was indeed shaped largely as a response to Israel's trauma in Babylon, we shouldn't be surprised to find hints of that here and there—with maybe a jab or two taken at their captors in the process.

For example, Israel's Babylonian captors were big on astrology, and the sun, moon, and stars might have been gods, though that is not clear. What *is* clear is that the heavenly bodies were thought to tell the future to those skilled enough to know how to read them. But for the Israelites, the heavenly bodies serve no such function. Instead they are "for signs and for seasons and for days and for years" (v. 14). That means they are there to mark the passing of time, not predict what is to come.

Also, "season" is the same word used a bunch of times in the Pentateuch to refer to "appointed times" of Israel's religious festivals commanded by God (one example is Exodus 23:15).

In other words, the heavenly bodies are put into place by God to keep track of how the Israelites are to worship him. Compared to what the Babylonians and other ancient peoples thought, Israel's God knocked the heavenly bodies down to size.

Another knock on the Babylonians and other religions was that Israel's God works solo. In the Babylonian story *Enuma*

Elish, we have a soap opera instead. The god Marduk has a longstanding grievance with his great-grandmother Tiamat. Apparently, this dysfunctional divine family didn't believe in counseling, so they settled their differences by Marduk cutting Tiamat in half (actually, fileting her top to bottom). With half her body, he made the barrier to separate the waters (the "firmament" of Genesis). But Israel's God is the great and mighty God. He created the cosmos solo and effortlessly, no debate and no battle, while the Babylonian creation story looks like a Jerry Springer episode.

Also, humans are created as God's crowning achievement. It is only following Day 6 that God declares what he has made "*very* good" (not simply "good" as in previous days). That's because humans bear God's likeness and image. In the ancient world, kings would put images of themselves in remote parts of their kingdom so that his subjects would know that he is still "there" even if he is far away. Also, kings were considered divine image bearers, governing the people in God's place.

In Genesis 1, all humans have this same royal status; they represent God in the world by ruling over all of creation in God's place:

> God blessed [humans] and said to them, "Be fruitful and multiply, and fill the earth and subdue it; and have dominion over the fish of the sea and over the birds of the air and over every living thing that moves upon the earth." (Genesis 1:28)

In fact, humanity's status is so high that later Jews (well after the Babylonian exile) wrote stories about how angry the angels were that humans were given such status that rivaled their own. This is even hinted at in the Bible itself: "What are mere mortals that you are mindful of them, human beings that you care for them? You have made them a little lower than the heavenly beings [angels] and crowned them with glory and honor" (Psalm 8:4–5).

This does not sound like other creation stories of the

ancient world. In the Babylonian creation story, humans are not made in God's image. In one story called the *Epic of Atrahasis*, humans were created as an afterthought to do the grunt work the gods are too good for or are simply too lazy to do. The elevation of humans as a whole, male and female, to the level of divine image bearer is an ancient Israelite comment on human equality. Maybe being captive in a foreign country gave them something to think about.

Genesis 1 is an ancient statement of faith that the God of Israel alone is worthy of Israel's worship. As tempting as it may be to follow the gods of the stronger nations, Genesis 1 puts the brakes on and says that this one God of a captive people is responsible for taming chaos and filling the air, sea, and earth. Such faith would encourage the Israelites to remain faithful to God even when the outlook wasn't that good.

In other words, Genesis 1 was not written to answer our curiosities about how the universe came to be. It was not written in code to show us that the Israelites had a basic grasp of the Big Bang, expanding universe, and Einstein's theory of relativity. Obviously, no ancient person would have understood those notions. Rather, it was written to tell the Israelites that their God, and not the gods of the other nations, is the chaos tamer. And they made this point on ancient terms, using ancient ways of thinking.

When the Babylonians had stories about angry gods conspiring against each other and cutting each other in half, the Israelites did not respond, "Oh, you Babylonians and your silly stories. Don't you know all this talk about the gods is just plain primitive?! Don't you know that there really is no solid structure above the earth keeping the water at bay? Don't you know that the stars are actually billions of light-years away, that the earth is a round ball and revolves around the sun, and that the universe is expanding at an amazing rate? Really! I mean, get with it!"

Instead the Israelites used the view of the universe they *shared* with their contemporaries to make a *unique* declaration of faith: "Our God, regardless of what you might think of us, a captured people, is not weak. He is, in fact, stronger than all your gods put together."

Later, in the exodus story, we will see one other rallying cry for the Israelites: "Not only is he the *creator*, but he is the *deliverer*, too." Yahweh as creator and deliverer are the two things that marked Israel's God off from all the others gods, and this is why he alone could expect Israel's undivided devotion. This is why worshiping the gods of other nations was as bad a thing as the Israelites could do, even if people of other nations changed gods like we change phone companies. Genesis 1 makes the case that abandoning Israel's God is to abandon the creator himself.

Cut the Israelites Some Slack

Sometimes modern readers of Genesis 1 think the story is a quaint relic of a silly ancient culture. Others, because it is part of the Bible, think that Genesis 1 has to be scientifically and historically accurate. Both ways of thinking sell the Bible short. Genesis 1 describes the cosmos in ancient terms—which should make sense to us, since the book was written by and for ancient Israelites.

One good example of how Genesis reflects an ancient view of the world is on Day 2, when God creates the *sky*. But this isn't any sky we've ever experienced. This "sky" is apparently solid—the "firmament" we mentioned earlier. It is a vault or dome of some sort that separates the *waters above* the vault from the *waters below*. Think of trying to set up a flattened tent during a torrential (chaotic) downpour. To get some shelter, you wiggle inside and lie flat. Then, after some struggling, you prop up the roof with one big pole in the middle, then slightly shorter ones around the edges. Because of the tent roof, you are now in a safe, enclosed "bubble," protected from the "waters above."

Another good visual is to think of the "sky" here as the glass dome of a snow globe if the snow globe was dunked in a tub of water. The glass dome separates the "waters above" from the "waters below," leaving a habitable space for life. Similarly, this dome keeps the waters above from crashing down and reintroducing chaos where God had given order. (And in the stories we find in Jonah, Job, and the Psalms, this snow globe is kept from floating around aimlessly in the deep by the "pillars" or "mountains of the earth," or to go back to our other metaphor, "ancient tent poles.") Here in Genesis 1:2, God creates this vault to put the chaotic waters "in their place," so to speak, so order can arise. If you are having trouble visualizing what this "sky" looks like, take a minute and Google "Ancient Near East Cosmology."

Remember, to read this story through ancient eyes means forgetting about telescopes, complicated charts of outer space, and Einstein. What you could see is what you got. And if we didn't have modern technology, thinking of the world as a giant snow globe isn't a bad place to start. The earth looked to them like a flat disc. And above is what looks like a rounded dome (the sky) that begins and ends on the horizons. Since the sky was blue, it was thought that it was water kept in place by the dome. Below the earth was more water. And everything seemed to be held up by mountains or pillars of some sort.

It's really inconceivable that Genesis would open up with anything other than an ancient view of the world. Not only would a science textbook be dull, it would also have been literally nonsense to readers of the Bible for a few thousand years. Remember, the point of an *ancient story* is to *tell a story*, not to correct our views about the mechanics of the universe.

At the same time, we have to give the Israelites a lot of credit for producing such a literary gem that still holds trained Bible readers captive 2,500 years later. The opening chapter of the Bible is not just slapped together like a last-minute term paper. The story is subtle, challenging, and artistic; the theology is deep and, against the ancient backdrop, staggering. This stands to reason: storytellers, not historians, scientists, or academics, produced this book.

Our world would be a much poorer place if we watched every movie pointing out all the ways in which Middle-Earth (from *The Lord of the Rings*) doesn't measure up to our modern ways of seeing the world. We have all experienced that annoying friend who keeps saying things like, "Oh brother, that would never happen in real life," during movies. Such a friend is missing the point. (Side note: if you haven't experienced that annoying friend, you probably *are* that annoying friend.) Stories are not waiting to be molded to fit our experience. They are waiting for us to take the risk of entering the world of the story and be changed by it.

With this we leave the first chapter of the Bible very much aware that we have only scratched the surface of things. But to read Genesis 1 as an ancient story of Israelite faith amid difficult times is a great place to start, and it is necessary preparation for reading the rest of Genesis.

Masaccio's "The Expulsion from the Garden of Eden" 15th century
Public Domain

4

Genesis 2-4: Adam Is Israel

When we move from Genesis 1 to Genesis 2–4, better known as the story of Adam and Eve, we might have a feeling of déjà vu. How can Genesis 2 be the "account of the heavens and the earth when they were created" (2:4)? Weren't the heavens and earth created in Genesis 1? Even before the time of Jesus, people noticed that Genesis 2 looks like a second creation account.

The problem, though, is that there are some clear differences between these two accounts. For example, in Genesis 1, vegetation is created on Day 3 (1:12–13) and humans are created on Day 6 (1:26–27). But in Genesis 2, humans are created before vegetation (2:5–9). Another difference is how and when people were created. In Genesis 1, all the animals are created first and then humans are created, both male and female together (1:24–27), as the crowning achievement of creation, made in God's image. But in Genesis 2, only one man, Adam, is created (2:7), then all the animals, which Adam names (2:19–20). When it was clear that no suitable "partner" for Adam could be found among them, only then does God create the woman from Adam's side (2:21–25).

And if we take a step back from the details, we see that not just the order of events is different—the whole "feel" of Genesis 2 is different. In Genesis 1, God is a high and lofty sovereign who moves things around like the cosmos is a chessboard. In Genesis 2, God is more human-like, he is more involved in the action on the ground, even taking a stroll in his private garden in the evening (3:8).

Why do we have two *very different* creation stories side-by-side at the very beginning of the Bible? Is someone trying to confuse us? Or did the writer of Genesis make a mistake? No, probably not. As we will see a little later in Genesis, when the writer puts together two stories that appear similar but are really quite different, each has a different purpose. Genesis 1 and 2, though similar, are different because they are talking about two different things. If we try to reconcile the differences by harmonizing these two chapters, we will miss the point. Instead, we should understand the distinct point each is making.

We looked at Genesis 1 in the last chapter. So what's up with Genesis 2? What is this story trying to say?

> Genesis 2 is not another version of the creation of the cosmos. It shifts the focus to the story of Israel.

Genesis 2 is actually the older of the two stories, probably written early in Israel's history when Israel still had kings—centuries before the Babylonian exile. Genesis 1, even though it comes first in our Bible now, was written later with the Babylonian exile in mind, as we saw last chapter. When the Bible was put together as we know it today, Genesis 1 was made the grand introduction to Israel's story: the God of Israel is the *true* creator of all things, the master chaos-tamer. Whereas Genesis 1 sets up the big picture, Genesis 2 moves quickly to the real heart of the Pentateuch and the whole Old Testament, the story of

Israel as God's people.

We know. It sounds awfully weird to think that the story of Adam and Eve is about Israel. Israel isn't even mentioned, for goodness sake. Well, that's why we're writing this chapter, to explain all this.

If we read the story carefully, keeping our ancient eyes open, we will see that there is more going on than we might be used to seeing with modern eyes. We will see that the story is the story of Israel in miniature. Wait! Before you think we are crazy, hang with us. We didn't cook this idea up ourselves. Ancient readers and modern scholars alike have seen it, too. To see why, we have to jump ahead in the story for just a minute, to the story of Adam's son, Cain.

Cain Is Not Alone

Cain's story (4:1–26) shows us that Genesis 2–4 is not about the creation of the first humans.

After Cain kills his brother Abel and is found out, God banishes him to become "a fugitive and a wanderer on the earth" (v. 12). In response, Cain becomes paranoid, afraid that "anyone who meets me will kill me" (v. 12). So God puts a mark on Cain's head to let everyone know to keep their hands off. Cain is satisfied with that, wanders off, and settles in the land of Nod (which means "wandering" in Hebrew), east of Eden (yes, that's where the Steinbeck novel and James Dean movie title come from). He finds a wife, settles down, has kids, and builds a city (v. 17).

If you have ever read this story to inquisitive children, you know what's coming next—the dreaded question that terrified Sunday School teachers pray is never asked: "Where did Cain get his wife from?" (*I don't know, Jimmy. Ask your parents.*) Along with that question, we can also add, "Where did this posse come from that Cain is so afraid of, and why exactly would one man in exile build a city?"

Even children recognize that if Adam and Eve were the

first humans, and Cain and Abel were their children, and if Abel is dead—that leaves three people on earth. So Genesis 4 just drops a bunch of other people in our laps without bothering to explain where they came from.

Some, who still want to read Genesis 2–4 as another account of creation, find an answer in Genesis 5:4, where we learn that Adam had "other sons and daughters." So, are we supposed to believe that Cain married his sister? Besides the fact that that's gross and a little creepy, let's also remember the story doesn't say that (or even suggest it). And besides, Genesis 5:4 seems to say that these other children were born after Seth, Adam and Eve's replacement child for Abel—all of that happened *after* the banishment of Cain and his marriage to his mysterious wife. And finally, think about this: for Cain to find a wife among his sisters while wandering around as a fugitive would mean that at least one sister (actually, a lot of brothers and sisters, since Cain builds a city) would have been banished, too. But again, the story doesn't say any of that.

Here's a simpler explanation: *there were other people living outside of the Garden of Eden all along*, even if the story doesn't explain it. Which leads to this: Maybe the story of Adam and Eve isn't about the first human beings. Maybe it's about something else. And that something else is this: *The Adam story is a story of Israel in miniature, a preview of coming attractions.*

Adam Is Israel

Try to forget what you know about the Adam story and look at the basic plot line. Adam is created by God outside of the garden and then put into a garden *paradise* (Eden means something like "abundance"). When he enters this paradise, he is given a *command* to follow—not to eat of the tree of the knowledge of good and evil. *On the day* he eats of it, God warns, Adam will die (2:17).

So far so good, but notice what happens on the day Adam eats the forbidden fruit: he doesn't die. In fact, Adam lives to the ripe old age of 930. So, what does it mean to die "on the day" he eats of it? Death means that Adam and Eve are *driven out of the garden* and not allowed to return, lest they eat of the tree of life (3:22–24).

"Death" in the Adam story has a double meaning. It means physical death, because being banished from the garden means they *no longer have free access to that other tree we read about, the tree of life*. That is the tree that keeps them from dying. So, in a way, Adam and Eve "die" physically by being evicted from paradise—they can't keep eating the fruit that gives the immortality, and so mortality is introduced: they will eventually return to dust (3:19).

But death also has another meaning, a metaphorical meaning: to be *exiled* from paradise is "death" for Adam. In Ezekiel 37, we see the same connection between death and exile. The prophet Ezekiel has a vision of a valley of dry bones—a mass, uncovered grave. The bones represent Israel in exile in Babylon. But then these bones are brought back together, covered with muscle and flesh, and God breathes life back into them (vv. 7–9).

Why would Israelites say that exile is death? Exile was not like being relocated today. Israel was a people of the land, the very land God gave them as a gift. In 2 Samuel 7, God promised that they would have the land as God's gift forever, and have a descendant of David sitting on the throne. But in exile, all that was gone—including the Temple, where Israel went to communicate with God and make sacrifices for the forgiveness of sins. Being in exile was a big deal. It meant the Israelites were completely cut off from God. They felt God had rejected them; he had finally turned his back and walked away.

Without God, Israel is no longer the people of God. Israel ceases to exist. Israel is dead. In Ezekiel, bringing the bones back to life represents Israel returning from captivity. Israel is restored, re-connected with God. Israel is brought back to life. Like Israel in exile, Adam *did* die the day he ate the fruit—he, too, was exiled (from Eden). Adam and Israel share the same fate.

But the parallel between Adam and Israel doesn't end

there. The stories of Adam and Israel follow the same plot line. Think about it.

Adam was *created* by God and *exiled* from *paradise* for disobeying the *command.*

Israel was *created* by God and *exiled* from *Canaan* for disobeying the *Law of Moses.*

Israel was "*created*" by God, beginning with Abraham, and then especially when delivered from the "dust" of slavery (it was a long process). God then took the Israelites to Mt. Sinai where, through Moses, he gave them *commands* to follow. He placed them in the land of Canaan, a land "flowing with milk and honey," which means the land was lush with two valuable sources of abundance and life in the ancient world: cattle and agriculture ("honey" means fruit nectar).

As long as Israel obeyed God's law given to Moses—especially the parts about having no other gods but Yahweh—it would go well for them in the land. But Israel had a long habit of worshipping other gods. After several centuries of this, God finally drove Israel into exile in Babylon.

Adam and Israel were both created by God and given a great plot of land to live on as long as they obeyed God. The Adam story isn't about "humanity" and it isn't supposed to be read as history or science—what modern eyes tell us. It is to be read through ancient eyes. The Adam story is a preview of Israel's story, which is what the Old Testament as a whole is about.

Now, let's come at this same idea but from a different angle.

Naïve Adam and Eve

Many Christians are taught to read the Adam and Eve story something like this: Adam and Eve are fresh-off-the-assembly line, shiny, new, perfect, first human beings—sort of super humans. God tested these flawless creatures with this command not to eat of the tree of the knowledge of good and evil, just to see if they meant business and would obey him. But they failed the test, rebelled against God, and lost not only their own perfection but also that of every other human being born since.

This way of understanding the Adam story has been popular for a very long time in Western Christianity, ever since St. Augustine (A.D. 354–430). But not everyone has read the story like this. The whole Eastern wing of the Church (Greek Orthodox is the major example) looks at the Adam story from a different angle. For them, the Adam story is not about a *fall down* from perfection, but a failure to *grow up* to godly wisdom and maturity.

Adam and Eve weren't like perfect super humans. They were like young, naïve children, who were meant to *grow* into obedience, but were tricked into following a different path. Why in the world would anyone read the Adam story this way? Well, as we are about to see, tons of reasons—and they all help us see that we are actually reading the story of Israel.

Look at the command God gave Adam. He can eat of any tree of the garden, any tree at all, except one: the tree of the knowledge of good and evil.

This raises an obvious question: Why that tree? How about a command not to eat from the tree of death and disease? Or the tree of sexual lust and lying? Why the tree of the knowledge of good and evil? What exactly is *wrong* with knowing the difference between good and evil? Did we miss something here? Isn't that what every parent wishes for his or her child? (Parents who worry about their teenagers, you know what we mean.) Why does eating from a tree that gives you the knowledge of good and evil carry the death penalty?

If this is a story about the first humans, this part of the story sticks out like a sore thumb. But if we think of the Adam story as a preview of the story of Israel, it makes a lot of sense.

Knowing the difference between good and evil is *the* point of the law in the Old Testament. The law, given to Moses at Mt. Sinai, tells Israel what is good and what is evil. And if they obeyed what the law says, it went well with them, which we already saw means that they would be able to stay in the land. If they disobeyed, it would lead to consequences, ultimately exile from the land. This is the big choice Israel faces throughout its history: obey the law and be blessed with land, disobey and forfeit the land.

The entire book of Proverbs is based on a similar idea, although it is described a bit differently. The book of Proverbs, before we get to all of those wonderfully pithy wise sayings, takes nine chapters setting up a similar choice. Israel is advised in Proverbs to follow *wisdom* and to flee from *foolishness*. What is wisdom? Obeying God and following his instruction (Proverbs 1:7). Following the path of God leads to wisdom and life (8:35) but following foolishness leads to death (8:36). Knowing right from wrong, knowing wisdom from foolishness, is what was expected of Israel. And to gain that knowledge, they needed to *learn* to obey God. The book of Proverbs was written as sort of a training manual to do just that.

God didn't command Adam and Eve not to eat of the tree of the knowledge of good and evil because such knowledge is *wrong*. It's not that God doesn't *ever* want Adam and Eve to know good and evil. That is precisely what he *does* want for them—but they have to go about gaining such knowledge *his* way. Obedience to God is the prerequisite for knowing good and evil. Proverbs 1:7 puts it this way: *The fear the Lord is the beginning of knowledge; fools despise wisdom and instruction.*

To use the language of Proverbs, Adam and Eve were fools. They spurned God's instruction and took the short cut to get to what was intended to be a good thing. But true knowledge can only be gained by submitting to God, trusting, revering, and loving him (all included in that phrase "fear the Lord"). And following God's path to wisdom brings *life,* which is what we read in Proverbs 3:18, "She [Wisdom] is a tree of life to those who lay hold of her." Pursuing wisdom God's way leads to a "tree of life"—for Israel and for Adam. Failure to follow God's path to wisdom leads to death, the estrangement from God, exile for Israel and for Adam.

Here's where the serpent comes in (3:1–7). He is

described as "more *crafty* than any other animal that the Lord God had made" (v. 1). That's not just a snappy way to introduce a character in a story. In Proverbs 1:4, we read that God's wisdom gives "*shrewdness* to the simple." "Shrewdness" in Proverbs and "crafty" in Genesis are the same Hebrew word. In English, crafty is the negative way of putting it and shrewdness is the positive way. Think of shrewdness as "street smarts." Someone who is shrewd won't be taken in by every shell game and card trick he passes on the street corner. Much of Proverbs is about preparing the young, the simple, the naïve, to make it in the world, where around every corner there is a potential temptation to drive you away from wisdom (and life) and toward foolishness (and death).

The brief dialogue that follows the serpent's entrance shows the *crafty* serpent outwitting *simple* Eve like a veteran car salesman manipulating a young first-time buyer with a wad of cash. As most of us have learned the hard way, car salesmen know more about why we buy cars than we do—they study it, go to seminars, practice it. They are crafty. They look for a way into your head to get you to buy a car you may not really want, can't afford, with features and warranties you might not need, and leave you feeling good and thinking it was all your idea . . . until the payment booklet arrives and reality sets in. The buyer must truly beware. If you are naïve, it is best that you don't "have a seat" at the desk and "crunch some numbers" at all. Just keep away—and whatever you do, keep your mouth shut.

The serpent is the crafty salesman and Eve the naïve customer. The serpent gets her talking and within two verses he has her wrapped around his finger and doubting God. "Trust me, lady. God's lying to you. He's even a bit jealous. The reason God doesn't want you to eat of that wonderful, beautiful, delicious tree is because he knows that when you eat from it you will become God-like yourselves, knowing good and evil."

A clever half-truth. Yes, if they eat of the tree they *will* be like God, *which is exactly what God wants.*

God wants his human creatures to look more and more like him, but the wise God must lead them in his way, in his time.

They are not ready to know good and evil. We all know from the classic Tom Hanks movie *Big* what happens when we "grow up" without all the experiences that come with maturity. In the same way, the serpent tricks naïve Eve to grab for wisdom by bypassing God's instruction—to grab for a good thing the wrong way.

After they eat, Adam and Eve instantly become aware of their nakedness and are ashamed. Of all things that could have happened, the earth opening up and swallowing them whole, being struck down dead by fire from heaven, why this? It's almost like some uptight conservatives wrote this story. But that's not what's happening here.

Think of young children. They tend to run around the house naked, without a care in the world. In fact, our kids would even literally run *around* the house naked, completely oblivious to the embarrassment they were heaping on their parents as the neighbors helplessly looked on. Children are naïve, simple. They don't know they are supposed to feel shame. But imagine what would happen if, while your child was running amok, you could give him a magic cookie that would instantly give him the understanding of a 21-year-old, bypassing years of growth and experiences that slowly matured him. Most likely, he would immediately scream, run into the bedroom, lock the door and find something to put over his private parts—like the fig leaves Adam and Eve used.

The serpent tricked Adam and Eve into gaining wisdom too soon, apart from God's way. They were naïve children who did not have the shrewdness to withstand the serpent's craftiness. They should have just trusted their maker. The knowledge of good and evil isn't wrong, but getting it free from God's direction is death. Without the maturity that comes from obeying God, Adam and Eve *can't handle the truth* (said in our best Jack Nicholson voice).

The Point

This is the point of this story: the choice put before Adam and Eve is the same choice put before Israel every day: *learn to listen to God and follow in his ways and then—only then—you will live*. The story of Adam and Eve makes this point in the form of a story; Proverbs makes it in the form of wisdom literature; Israel's long story in the Old Testament makes it in the form of history writing.

The story of Adam and Eve is a preview of Israel's long journey in the Old Testament as a whole.

Adam did not get back into the garden, but the Old Testament does not dwell on that story. In fact, Adam is not mentioned again in the Old Testament except for 1 Chronicles 1:1, where he is the first name in the long nine-chapter list of names. The Old Testament focuses on Israel itself. And Israel does come back to the garden, back to Canaan, in 539 B.C. after about fifty years of captivity in Babylon. As Ezekiel wrote, the death of exile is reversed and Israel's dead bones are brought back to life. Israel's estrangement from God is over. As the prophet Isaiah puts it, "[Jerusalem] has served her term, her penalty is paid, she has received from the Lord's hand double for all her sins" (40:2).

At the end of the day, Israel's story is less about the people and more about the God who never fully lets go them, always moving to bring them back to paradise.

William Blake's "The Murder of Abel," 18th century
Public Domain

5

Genesis 4-5: Cain Is a Fool

Things started off so well. Israel's God orders the cosmos singlehandedly and puts Adam and Eve, his special people, in a garden paradise. We should all have it so good. But by the time we get to Genesis 3, we have a series of problems on our hands. Adam and Eve are exiled from paradise, with armed and loaded angels guarding the way back (3:24). The big question at this point is: What will happen next? Where will they go? What will they do? And will things get any worse?

Why yes—yes they will. Genesis 4 introduces us to Adam's sons, Cain and Abel, a story we glimpsed in the previous chapter. Cain, the older, will quickly follow in his parents' foolish footsteps. His, too, is a story where disobedience leads to death and discord.

Like Father, Like Son

The story begins with some things that come out of nowhere. Cain and Abel each present a *sacrifice* and God accepts one and rejects the other. This favoritism prompts Cain to be angry toward his little brother. Okay, but how did Cain and Abel even know what sacrifice was and how to do it? And why in the world would God be angry about one type of sacrifice and not the other? Somebody throw us a bone here. Well, this is a puzzle—unless we remember that we are reading a story of Israel in miniature, just like the story of Adam and Eve.

The key here is the kind of sacrifices Cain and Abel offer: pastoral and agricultural. We will read later in the Old Testament that God commanded the Israelites to offer the firstborn of their *flock* (Exodus 13:12) and the first fruit of their *produce* (Leviticus 23:10). This story is written for Israel and these later commands are in the background of the Cain and Abel story. The problem with Cain is that he did not offer specifically the *first fruit* of the harvest, just a plain old "offering of fruit" (Genesis 4:3). That is, just like Adam and Eve, Cain has broken God's law. God, therefore, favors Abel's offering but rejects Cain's.

Cain is not happy about this at all. God saw his unhappiness (and perhaps his growing resentment) and told Cain that if he had offered a better sacrifice, he wouldn't have this problem. He also told him that "sin is lurking at the door; its desire is for you, but you must master it" (4:7). In other words, "Your anger is your own fault, and you'd better hold it in check or something terrible will happen." But, like his parents, Cain played the fool, ignored God's warning, and killed his brother in a premeditated fit of jealousy. Like his parents, Cain chose death—though this time failing to follow God's way leads to murder.

How is this the story of Israel in miniature? Well, we saw in the last chapter that the Adam story mirrors Proverbs. So does the Cain story.

In Proverbs, right after we are told how great wisdom is (1:1–7), we move right into a warning about murder. Specifically, the "son" who is being instructed in Proverbs is warned not to give in to sin (v. 10)—specifically, not to go along with those sinners who entice you to "Come with us, let us lie in wait for blood; let us wantonly ambush the innocent" (v. 11).

Of all the things to bring up at the very beginning of Proverbs, why murder? Because the story of Cain and the wisdom sayings of Proverbs are two versions of the same story: be wise by following God's commands and you get life, or be foolish by rejecting God's commands and you get death. Failure to follow wisdom has its lethal consequences—not only privately, but socially.

Exile Is Just the Beginning

The blood of Abel cries out to God and Cain is punished. Cain will no longer be a farmer but must now be a "restless wanderer." Adam and Eve were exiled from the garden. But now Cain is exiled from God's very presence and begins cavorting with the people of Nod. (In the last chapter, we looked at who these other people were.)

The first thing we are told is that Cain has sex with his wife and has a son they name Enoch. Then Cain builds a *city* for Enoch, even though God told him to be a *wanderer.* Not only that, but in the ancient world of the Old Testament (though not in the Old Testament itself), building cities is usually something that the gods are known for. Cain surely seems to be hitting one minefield after another. He has "wandered" far from the path of the creator, that's for sure.

The story moves quickly from Enoch to Enoch's great-great-grandson Lamech, and things keep going downhill. We are introduced to Lamech as the first polygamist (he marries two women). Lamech then has three sons who become "fathers of industry." Jabal is the father of people who dwell in tents and raise livestock (what a legacy); Jubal, the father of all who play the harp and flute; and Tubal-Cain, the first to forge tools out of bronze and iron.

While his sons were busy inventing tools and musical instruments, Lamech was out killing a man—just like his great-great-grandfather, Cain. And Lamech arrogantly thinks he can force God's hand, saying that if Cain was protected in his murderous ways, so will he be, and even more so. The story leaves off there abruptly, but we are left thinking to ourselves, "Who does this guy think he is?" We are also given a pretty strong hint that the line of Cain is majorly screwed up. Cain's descendants are moving further and further from God's ways.

Remember, Genesis 2–4 is not a story of the *ultimate* origin of *everything*. It's clear this writer has an agenda to tell the story of Israel's relationship with God, with no space to waste on other matters, like what other people were doing at the time. Cain and his line are a train wreck—they exemplify what happens to a people who are utterly cut off from God. The family tree of Israel does not concern Cain's family. But then who? Abel is dead. Who is left?

We get an answer in Genesis 4:25. While Cain's family is busy building cities and tools, Adam and Eve have another son to replace Abel and name him Seth. Seth has a son named Enosh, and with that birth we have a key moment in the story: Seth does not build Enosh a city like Cain does for Enoch. Instead, when Enosh is born, "at that time people began to call on the name of Yahweh" (4:26). That is a good Old Testament way of saying that when Seth is born, people begin worshiping Yahweh.

The line of Seth may not be perfect, as we will see again and again in Genesis. But at least they are calling on Yahweh's name. Seth's line will eventually bring us to Abraham, the father of Israel, the people of Yahweh.

No, You May Not Skip These Names

With all this action going on, we might come to Genesis 5

and think it's an intermission. "A list of names? Really? I'm supposed to read that?" Some of us can't even name all of our cousins, so who needs a list of people you don't know? You might have grown up thinking that "so and so begat so and so" was another way of saying "skip this section, it's not important and will just make you insecure because of all the names you can't pronounce." But, in the Bible, these family trees are more than just an excuse to get up and go to the bathroom. So skip over them if you must. We can't force you to listen. But we want you to feel just a little bit guilty about it.

While we might find it boring to read another family's genealogy, most people find their own family history at least a little interesting. People often wear their ancestors like a badge of honor, finding it meaningful that they are a part of George Washington's or Abraham Lincoln's family tree. Biblical genealogies remind Israel they are part of the family tree whose roots are firmly planted in a relationship with their creator and redeemer. They are major moments in Genesis that connect the past with the present. It is a reminder that they are still connected to the people of God from way back.

Side note: The clearest example of this, if you want to flip there, is the genealogy in the first nine chapters of 1 Chronicles. Talk about a snooze, but this genealogy was a big deal. It was written long after the Israelites returned from exile, when people were fretting over where they stood as a people with God. Those nine chapters of [yawn] names end with the returnees from exile—and it all begins with Adam in 1 Chronicles 1:1. This genealogy is saying, "We are still the people of God, just like we have always been, from the very beginning."

The genealogy in Genesis 5 connects Israel to its past, but it also moves us forward to where the story is headed. Chapter 5 begins with our second "this is the account of" phrase, so it introduces a new section of Genesis. The genealogy is like a map, making sure we know that the story is headed down Seth's line, not Cain's. It is the line of Adam through Seth that is close to God, not the line of Cain that gives us people like the arrogant, murderous Lamech.

The genealogy also lets us move quickly to the next scene—like when movies skip over a lot of time by saying "five years later." We start chapter 6 hundreds of years after the end of chapter 4, and chapter 5 gets us there.

But one thing about this list of names that jumps out at you is how long the people live—almost 1,000 years each. That's an awfully long time. The famous Methuselah gets the prize for living the longest, 969 years old. Adam did pretty well for himself, too, living 930 years. Seth was 912, and so on. The only ones who did not break the 900-year barrier were Mahalalel (a mere 895 years), Lamech (777 years, no relation to Cain's Lamech), and Enoch.

This Enoch, of no relation to Cain's Enoch, doesn't die at all. He inexplicably "walked with God; then he was no more, because God took him" (Genesis 5:24). It would be nice if the writer filled us in a little about Enoch, like what he did differently than everybody else, and what it means for God to "take" him and for him to be "no more." Maybe everyone knew about Enoch and needed no further explanation, which is another reminder to us (as if we needed it) that we are modern people reading ancient texts.

What accounts for people living so long? To understand, we have to get rid of our idea of genealogies as we know them today. That means we shouldn't be calculating the age of the earth using these genealogies, as Anglican bishop James Ussher did back in the seventeenth century. He decided, based on these genealogies, that the earth was created Sunday, October 23, 4004 B.C. A careful study of biblical genealogies—and genealogies of the ancient world in general—shows that they do have a point to make, but an accurate historical timeline isn't it.

We need to read these long life spans with ancient eyes. It helps to know that Israel's neighbors used big numbers in similar ways, which we can see in an ancient text known as the "Sumerian King List." This is a list of kings who each ruled for thousands of years before the flood, the longest reign being 65,000 years, but ruled a mere 900 years or so after the flood. The ages in Genesis 5 may be more "reasonable," but they still aren't telling us how long people lived. Both the Sumerian King List and Genesis are using the idea of superhuman lifespans to say that the flood was a major shift in the human drama. Death came much more slowly back then.

We end the family line of Seth with the birth of Noah. Genesis 5:29 describes him this way: "Out of the ground that the Lord has cursed this one shall bring us relief from our work and from the toil of our hands." That's quite a son. And all sorts of flares and firecrackers should be shooting off inside of our brains. Noah is born to reverse the curse of Adam, where the ground was cursed and which resulted in great toil and labor (3:17–19). God is about to do something new through Noah, a second Adam.

But this will be no stroll in the park. Things are about to get chaotic (literally). In an ancient sense of the word, all hell is about to break loose.

Daniel Maclise's "Noah's Sacrifice,"
19th century Public Domain

6

Genesis 6-9: Everyone Is Annihilated

The most familiar parts of the Bible are often the parts we have the hardest time reading through ancient eyes. And everyone is familiar with the story of the flood: Noah, the ark, animals marching on two-by-two—basically the life-blood of every Sunday school class flannel graph and coloring page. We suppose it can't be helped. After all, animals on a boat with a rainbow above seem friendly enough. Plus, the story comes with a nice lesson about God's faithfulness.

Only, it's not a children's story, and the way it is presented to children tames it to the point of distortion. The flood story isn't an ancient version of *Bambi* or *The Lion King*. It's more like *28 Days Later* or *Contagion*.

The flood story is a horrific moment in Genesis. The human experiment has failed, and apparently the only possible solution open to God was to kill every living thing, by drowning all things, save for one family and a limited number of animals. Why would a loving God, and master designer of the cosmos, do such a thing?

This is one of those stories where leaving the modern world behind is absolutely necessary. We might want to read this story as a scientific account of the past, arguing whether it was a global flood or a local flood, or wondering if the extinction of dinosaurs can be chalked up to a lack of room on the ark. But none of these questions helps us see the story as ancient Israelites would have seen it.

The Question Is Why, Not How

The first thing that helps us take off our modern glasses is to recognize that (1) Israel's neighbors also had flood stories very similar to the biblical one, and (2) Israel's flood story was written after these other stories (as we saw with the creation story in Genesis 1). These older versions come from ancient Sumeria, Assyria, and Babylon. It seems there really was a catastrophic flood at some point in the far distant past (some archaeologists say around 2900 B.C.) in the ancient Near East. *And different cultures in that region gave different reasons for why it happened.*

In other words, a massive, memorable, flood was an actual historical event, but the ancient stories were about *why* it happened, not *what* happened. And in the ancient world, there was no doubt that a major catastrophe like this happened for some divine reason.

Let's remember that ancient peoples, including the Israelites, had no notion of a round globe. Their world was flat. So when the Bible says that the "earth" was corrupt and that the "earth" was flooded, we can't picture "earth" as the blue marble moving through the solar system. They simply weren't aware of what the earth looked like as we see it today. For them, "earth" was what they could see from their earth-bound perspective. And from that perspective, the earth was flat and ended where the horizon ended (as it looks to any of us standing in the middle of a huge field out in the middle of nowhere).

If you put yourself in that world, the flood stories make more sense. You would have seen the rains pouring down for days upon days and the rivers rising until, slowly but surely, things are covered up and people die in masses. This is the flooding of their world. For *them* the flood was truly worldwide, but their "world" included only what they could see, what we might call the "known world."

As we said, the ancients were interested in *why* something like this could happen, specifically what role the gods played. Even though we are focusing on the ancient mindset, in a way, not much has changed. The tragic tsunami that took so many lives in 2006 brought many religious leaders and millions of religious and non-religious people to ask, once again, how can a supposedly good God let something like this happen? As religious people, we were not very interested in how it happened. We leave that to the scientists. We are much more invested in why it would happen in the creation of a good God. We are asking what catastrophes like this mean.

Ancient writers each answered the why question differently, but there are still some similarities with the biblical story that make you do a double take. The two most relevant stories for Genesis were written in the Akkadian language (the great-grand-uncle of Hebrew and the language spoken by ancient Assyrians and Babylonians). We know these stories by the first name of the main characters, *Atrahasis* and *Gilgamesh*.

Two Very Old Flood Stories

Atrahasis is the name of this story's Noah figure. Why did

the flood happen in the story of *Atrahasis*? It's hard to sugarcoat this: the high god and god of weather, Enlil, wanted to destroy humans for making too much noise. Atrahasis, with the help of the water god Ea, escaped the wrath of Enlil by building a large boat in which to save humanity.

The other story's main character, Gilgamesh, was actually the name of a historical figure, the king of Uruk who lived around 2,500 B.C. The story about him, however, is completely fanciful. He was two-thirds god and one-third human and had regular dealings with the gods. After the death of his dear friend Enkidu, Gilgamesh takes a journey to find the secret of immortality. This quest leads him to Utnapishtim, this story's Noah figure. He had obtained immortality from the gods and Gilgamesh hoped he could tease the secret out of him. But he tells Gilgamesh that his immortality came through special circumstances: he was the sole survivor of a great flood. We aren't told in this story specifically what led to the flood, but we are told that the god Ea had second thoughts and told Utnapishtim to build a boat with specific dimensions and get as many animals on board as possible. He did and survived the flood, by the grace of Ea.

Some of the similarities between these two stories and Genesis are striking: the building of a large boat according to precise instructions and dimension; bringing animals on board as well as the family; sealing the door with pitch (tar); the boat coming to rest on a mountain; releasing birds to see if the waters had subsided. Typically, similarities like these don't mean that one writer copied from another written story. Often, stories were passed down orally and were simply "in the air," and people talked about them freely.

In the case of the flood story, however, Genesis looks so much like these other stories, especially *Gilgamesh*, that some sort of borrowing is not a far-fetched idea—the biblical writer may very well have taken some specific ideas from *Gilgamesh* and tweaked them for his story.

All of this reminds us that "reporting the facts of history" is not what is going on here in the various flood stories of the ancient world, even though a massive flood is the likely historical event that lies behind all of them. For ancient peoples, including the Israelites, the point was to use the flood as a platform to talk about how *they* saw the world and *their* place in it. For the Israelites it became a way of talking about their God—what makes him different from all the other gods, and therefore why he alone is worthy of their devotion.

Flood Story: Israelite Version

So how is Yahweh different in Genesis 6–9 than the other gods are in the other flood stories? We have already seen that in the *Atrahasis* story, the cause of the flood was that the gods had grown tired of how much noise these humans were making. Sure, humans were nice to have around to do the grunt work the gods didn't want to do, but, like the Grinch, all the noise down in Whoville was just getting to be too much.

But the cause of the flood in Genesis 6–9 goes in a radically different direction. The God of Israel is not the type of God who wipes out all of life because he needs to get more sleep. Israel's God has other reasons, and to understand them, we need to look at where the flood shows up in the course of the larger story.

The flood story begins in Genesis 6:1–4, one of the most curious passages in the Old Testament. There we read that the "sons of God" (heavenly beings of some sort) were having sex with human women whom they found attractive. Such crisscrossing of the divine and human realms is a common feature in ancient religions (think of Greek myths where gods and humans are having sex all the time). But not for Israel. The world that Israel's God created is not a revolving door between the divine and human realms. In God's world, things have their place, and divine beings cavorting with human women violates the *order of creation*—the order that God established in Genesis 1. The flood is partly a response to this utter disregard for the order of the cosmos that God set up.

Move to Genesis 6:5 and we have come to the last straw.

The wickedness among humans has gotten out of hand, and God regrets ever having made humans to begin with. (Yes, God regrets what he did. We see how "human" God acts here as he did in the Adam story—walking in the garden, interrogating Adam, that sort of thing.) It's time for a clean slate—to wipe out the cosmos and start again. Noah, however, is righteous and blameless (6:9 and 7:1). We are not told what he did to get such praise, but as a result he (and his family) get to escape. Every other human drowns, along with the animals (except for those who came aboard).

This sounds a bit harsh, but we have to look at the big picture with ancient eyes. The reason for the destruction of humanity (as hard as that might be for modern readers to swallow) was due to a failure on the part of humanity, from the very beginning, to follow through with the program and act like what they were created for—to follow God's ways that lead to life. Thus far nothing has gone right, and now we even have a breach between heaven and earth in Genesis 6:1–4. Humanity has chosen the path to death.

From our modern point of view—especially Christians with the gentleness of Jesus in our minds—God might look more like Megatron here than the God who so loved the world that he gave his only son (John 3:16). Is mass killing really the best way to address the problem? Couldn't God have found some other way? But we'll need to table that sort of thinking if we want to get to what is going on here.

Let's remember that for ancient Israel, as for other cultures, this deathly flood had to be explained *somehow*. And the Israelites gave an explanation that said something loud and clear about how their God was different from the other gods. Their God isn't touchy and grumpy; he has standards he expects his created beings to uphold. For God to have killed all life on earth must mean that his standards have been violated across the board. Or, as the writer of the story puts it, "every inclination of the thoughts of their hearts was only evil continually" (6:5). So, God wiped the slate clean and started over by choosing Noah, the righteous one, as the new beginning.

His story begins in Genesis 6:9 with the third "this is the account of" introduction, which will take us through Genesis 9 (the end of the flood story). Most people know their way around this story. God warns Noah of the impending doom and then tells him to build an ark the size of a shopping mall, according to a specific floor plan.

When Noah is finished, the animals come on board, two by two, as well as seven of each of the "clean" animals so that proper sacrifices could be made afterward. That little tidbit sort of jumps out. Where does the idea of clean animals come from? As we saw in the sacrifices made by Cain and Abel, this is a clue that the Israelite audience for this story already knew what this meant. The book of Leviticus, part of God's commands to Moses on Mt. Sinai, explains all of this: there are some animals God accepts for sacrifice (clean) and others he doesn't (unclean). Later Israelite reality is brought back into these stories about ancient times, long before Moses.

If Noah is a new beginning for God, it's not surprising that we find hints of the creation story in the flood story. Remember that on Day 1 of the creation story, there was a "deep," a chaotic mass of water that made the cosmos uninhabitable. On Day 2, God divided the waters (above and below) and created a dome to keep chaotic waters above from crashing back down on the earth and making it uninhabitable again. We don't find out until Genesis 7:11 that this dome came equipped with "windows," which come in handy if you are going to flood the earth and make it uninhabitable again. So, we read in Genesis 7:11 that "all the fountains of the great deep [the same deep God's spirit hovered over in Genesis 1:2] burst forth, and the windows of the heavens were opened."

The order that God established on Day 2 by putting the waters in their place is undone; God has reintroduced chaos. The cosmos is as it once was—formless and empty, *tohubohu*. And it's a fitting verdict. God is only giving humanity a dose of their own medicine. If his creation behaves in a "disorderly" and chaotic way, God will unleash the forces of chaos upon them to wipe the slate clean and introduce a new *order*. The flood may be a morally disturbing story for us today to get our arms around (and it is), but in the flow (pardon the pun) of the story thus far, it is *the* fitting way to address the problem.

The end of the flood story also reminds us of Genesis 1. After God promises not to flood the earth again and gives a sign of this promise by providing a rainbow, he then gives the command to be fruitful, increase, and fill the earth. Bells should be going off at this point. This is the command God first gave in Genesis 1:28. Noah, his sons, and all their wives are a new creation. God, through Noah, is saying, "Let's try this again."

To close out the story, God leaves the rainbow as a sign that he will never destroy the earth like this again—which sounds like God is a bit sorry for having gone overboard. But just to be clear, the rainbow is not the stuff of Precious Moments posters. The bow is a weapon, God's bow of warfare. Displaying the bow in the sky after a rain means he is hanging it up; no more warfare against his creation. As we will see beginning with Abraham, God will soon reveal a different strategy for addressing the problem of humanity.

Wicked, Evil Canaan

You might think that the survivors would breathe a sigh of relief and turn it around a bit and try harder to follow Noah's example and be righteous and blameless. If only. In a discouraging turn of events, we leave this section with our "new creation," this attempt to "start over," quickly turning sour in a very weird way.

After getting off the boat, Noah plants a vineyard. Innocent enough. But then he has a little too much to drink and passes out butt-naked in his tent. This is not a moral lesson about the evils of drinking wine. Actually, this isn't about Noah at all, but about his sons' reactions.

Noah has three sons—Shem, Ham (the youngest, pronounced "Hahm," not like the meat), and Japheth. Ham has the grave misfortune of discovering dad lying there naked. He goes out to tell his brothers. What an awkward conversation. His brothers have the sense to go back in with a blanket, walking backward out of respect, to cover up their father. Noah wakes up from his drunken stupor and finds out what happened. The retribution against Ham is swift, if also a bit over the top and misdirected. Does this really deserve a full-blown curse? Really? And wouldn't it have been better to curse Ham directly? Instead Noah curses Ham's son Canaan? Canaan's descendants will be slaves to the descendants of Shem and Japheth.

So, let's get this straight. The Canaanites as a people are cursed because their ancestor, Canaan's father Ham, saw his father Noah drunk and naked? Frankly, that is an odd direction to take the story of Noah—but here is another place where we have to remember that this is part of *Israel's* story told from a later point of view. The Canaanites play a major role in Israel's story, as Israel's archenemies. They live in the land God promised to Israel through Abraham (as we shall see). They are the people God commands the Israelites to exterminate after the exodus. They are the people who will be a continual thorn in Israel's side until they are finally driven out during the reign of Israel's hero, King David.

Also, think about Ham *seeing* the *nakedness* of his father. Ham's sin was not just any old sin that happened to strike the writer's fancy. The last time we saw that combination of words was when Adam and Eve *saw* they were *naked* after eating the forbidden fruit. The difference is that Adam and Eve were ashamed as a result, while Ham takes it all in stride and even goes out to tell his brothers. Remember that the shame of Adam and Eve came from the *knowledge* they received (too quickly) from eating from the tree of the knowledge of good and evil. Ham has no shame because he is a brute—he has no knowledge.

The flood story is Israel's vehicle for talking about how their God is different from the gods of the other nations. It is also a vehicle for the later Israelite writer to explain why the hated Canaanites deserved everything they got, including being exterminated from their homeland so it could be given to the Israelites: they have been an accursed race since the beginning—

because Ham saw Noah's nakedness.

We end this part of the story with Noah living to be 950 and the descendants of his three sons spread out over the known world. The command to be fruitful and increase in number is being realized, as we will see in the next chapter: a list of the nations that came to fill the world from Noah, seventy in all—a nice, round, perfect number.

Hendrick van Cleve's "The Construction of the Tower of Babel," 16th century Public Domain

7

Genesis 10-12: Babylon Is Evil

The story of Noah leads to another chapter of names we don't know. Before you skip this section (we know you want to), at least look at how it begins, with the fourth "this is the account of" section of Genesis. So, right there we know that these names are important enough to get their own section heading.

Remember that lists of names clearly meant something to the Israelites who recorded these stories. They were former captives in a foreign land, determined to remember that they were the people of Yahweh, despite the national tragedy of exile. This list of nations in chapter 10 recounts how the descendants of Noah's three sons spread out over the known world to become the various people groups of the ancient world. This genealogy shows that the Israelites, the descendants of Shem, were the center of God's plan after the flood.

The first son of Noah named is Japheth and fourteen nations are named that descend from him. They are said to occupy what is now parts of Turkey and Greece along with areas further north. Each of these fourteen nations has its own *language* (this detail will be important in a minute). Ham, mentioned second, is the dark ancestor of pretty much anyone who will give the Israelites some sort of trouble later on (thirty are mentioned in Genesis 10:6–20), including the Canaanites, Assyrians, and Babylonians. These latter two settle in *Shinar* (this will also be important in a minute). They, too, have their own group of *languages*.

Finally, Shem and his family are listed, also with their own languages. "Shem" is where the word "Semitic" comes from, which for us today has become a synonym for "Jewish." Here it refers to the people group from which the Israelites came. This list functions like the last list in Genesis 5. That list focused us on the story of Seth's family and fast-forwarded us to Noah. This list in chapter 10 focuses our attention on Shem's family, fast-forwarding us to Abraham, the central figure of Israel's humble beginnings.

But before we get to Abraham, as if to make a point one last time before moving on, the writer takes a slight detour to the land of Shinar and an ill-advised construction project.

Those Babylonians Again

We have a list of nations in chapter 10 and Abraham's family tree starting at Genesis 11:10. Sandwiched in between is a curious story that only takes up nine verses, a story that begins rather abruptly: "Now the whole world had one language and the same words."

Really? We just read, not five seconds ago in chapter 10, that there were three basic people groups, each with their own language (10:5, 20, 31), that were spread out as seventy nations all over the (known) world. What gives? Did the biblical writer not know he was putting a story in Genesis 10 that contradicted the next story in Genesis 11? Was he asleep at the editing table, or did he just have bad organizational skills? If he wanted to confuse us, mission accomplished.

But the writer is not trying to confuse anyone. He is trying to get the reader's attention, and putting these stories together like this is not an act of carelessness. To see the point, we must remember, once again, that Genesis was put together by Israelites who had been captured by the *Babyl*onians (as in the Tower of Babel-onians?).

Our little nine-verse interlude assumes the existence of one people with one language putting up stakes in the "plain of Shinar." Remember who settles in Shinar in chapter 10? Oh, just the Babylonians, the enemies of Israel who will later destroy their temple and take them to Babylon.

This post-flood group comes together to build a famous tower designed to reach into the heavens. This type of ancient structure is well known today because of the work of archaeologists. It's called a ziggurat, a common structure of worship in the ancient world. It looked like a pyramid with stairs for sides and an altar on top. Since the gods were up there somewhere, building a "stairway to heaven" was an attempt to get in touch with the gods. By contrast, Israel's worship structures (the tabernacle and later the temple) don't have steps going up to heaven. Instead, Israel waits for God to come down.

But the Babylonians had their share of ziggurats, and this story sure reads like a slam on their worship practices. In Israel's mind, it was evidence of Babylonian arrogance and pride to build a structure to heaven, as though you could get God's attention that way. God's response in this story is both comical and ironic. (1) This high-rise building, that supposedly reaches heaven, God has to come *down* to see (11:5). (2) They built it so that they would not scattered over the earth (11:4), yet that is exactly what happens.

The confusion of languages is a play on words. The Hebrew word for "confuse" is *balal*, which is a pun on the

Hebrew word *babel*, as in, the Tower of Babel. This is also where our word "to babble" comes from. This story does not give an historical account of where languages came from. It is brilliant political satire as we move to the story of Abraham. Those silly, stupid, arrogant Babylonians.

Also, think of this episode as the inverse of Genesis 6:1–4. There the sons of God break through the boundaries God set up for the cosmos and *come down*, with grave consequences. Now, these Babylonians are trying to break through the cosmic boundaries by *going up* to get to God's level. The Babylonians will later rebel against the true God when they sack God's house, the Temple in Jerusalem, and then carry Israel and the booty off to Babylon. This story is a way for later Israelites to say, "At it again, huh? We know all about you, Babylonians. We know how you began and it seems things haven't changed much."

Chapters 10 and 11 give us two different explanations for why people are spread out around the known world and speak different languages. The list of nations in chapter 10 shows the people spreading out throughout the world after the flood, just as they are supposed to do (9:1, 7). They are fruitful and multiplying, which yields seventy nations, a number of completion or perfection. Chapter 10 also takes a good swipe at one of Israel's later enemies, the Canaanites. The story of Babel paints the fact of national language differences in a bad light, blaming the Babylonians for this confusing mess. This story points a condemning finger at Babylon: "You have been an annoying, destructive, godless pain in the side from the beginning."

Failed Humanity, Meet Abraham

We are on the verge of something new yet again, another chosen one, Abram (later called Abraham), who will be the father of *one* nation, Israel. Genesis 1–11 as a whole has led us to this point. The world is a mess, but there is one line—to be traced from Adam to Seth to Noah to Shem and now to

Abraham—that God intends to use to clean up the mess. Or better, let's say that God is moving to order chaos once again, not as in the days of Noah by wiping the slate clean, but by working through a people, set apart for him, as were Adam and Noah.

Enter Abraham, whose story is introduced at the end of the account of Shem (11:10–26) in the fifth "this is the account of" section in Genesis. But we quickly move to the sixth "this is the account of" section in 11:27 with the account of Terah, Abraham's father. It seems like the writer is burning up his allotted ten "accounts" pretty early: six down and we're not even out of chapter 11. But this sixth section will take a while: we won't see another one until chapter 25. After all, the line of Terah is about Abraham, *the* central character in Genesis, and, along with Moses and King David, one of the three most central characters in the entire Old Testament.

Chapter 11 ends with Terah taking his family out of Ur (in Babylon) and moving them northwestward along the two rivers (Tigris and Euphrates) to Haran, north of the land of Canaan. The writer adds here that Abraham's wife Sarai (later called Sarah) is barren, which will become a key point in the story soon enough.

The preliminaries are over. The writer has taken eleven chapters preparing his readers to understand Israel's story. We now move to the beginning of the story of Israel as a nation, destined by God to be blessed by him and to be a blessing to the nations. At least, that's the plan. The rest of the Old Testament will go into great detail about the struggle between God and Israel as God tries to move Israel toward their calling.

Caravaggio's "The Sacrifice of Isaac,"
16th century Public Domain

8

Genesis 12-22: Abraham Is Chosen

We are at a major transition in the story of Genesis, and it's a good idea to take a minute and remember how important it is to put aside modern reading habits. Oftentimes we are taught to read the Bible the same way we read a book like *Aesop's Fables* or *The Adventures of Winnie-the-Pooh*—as a collection of short, stand-alone stories. These stories may have some of the same characters, but there is no ongoing story line. We should not bring that way of reading to the Bible, where we are left with the "story of Noah's ark" or the "story of Joseph" as stand-alone stories with moral lessons to be learned. These stories are part of a larger continuous story.

Genesis was not written like *Aesop* or *Winnie-the-Pooh*. It was written in the way of *Alice*. When we read *Alice's Adventures in Wonderland* to our kids, they always want to know what happens *next*, because they know each part hangs together as one story that will find its climax at the end of the whole book, not the end of a single episode. To think that we can fully understand the story of Abraham's sacrifice of Isaac in Genesis 22, for example, without reading the first twenty-one chapters of Genesis is like flipping to the tea party in *Alice* and thinking the "point" of that story is that we should never dine with someone who is crazy and wears mad hats.

Genesis is not a series of pithy short stories with moral lessons, but a series of vital stepping-stones in the story of Israel's beginnings.

We have purposely spent a lot of time in the first eleven chapters of Genesis. Sure, these chapters are some of the most controversial, but that's not why we've paid close attention. These chapters set up the story of Israel by telling the story of Israel in miniature form. Israel's story is set against a dark backdrop, where the world is clearly off kilter. Chaos continues to threaten the order of creation. In one horrific episode, God intends to start over with Noah, but that didn't do the trick. The question now is, what will happen next? What will God do? These are the questions we are left with as we end Genesis 11. The glimmer of hope is a family line that began with Adam, through Seth, and now Terah.

This glimmer becomes brighter as we turn to Genesis 12. God initiates a relationship with a resident of the city of Ur in Babylon, a man named Abram, who will later become Abraham. The writer of Genesis keeps our focus on Abraham until chapter 25, when he dies and the camera focuses on his son Isaac, and then Isaac's son Jacob, who will be renamed Israel. From Abraham's loins, God will make himself a people and eventually give them a land. God is making a nation and their destiny is to be the tool God uses to restore order to the chaos of chapters 3–11.

An Unlikely Hero

The story of Abraham starts abruptly, almost like we are

coming in on the middle of something. Genesis 12:1–3 starts,

> Yahweh said to Abram, "Go from your country and your people and your father's house to the land that I will show you. I will make you into a great nation and I will bless you and make your name great, so that you will be a blessing. I will bless those who bless you, and the one who curses you I will curse; and in you all the families of the earth shall be blessed."

Okay, but we are not told how a resident of Mesopotamia knew who Yahweh was. In fact, Joshua 24:2 hints that at least Terah, if not Abraham himself, was well acquainted with the worship of Mesopotamian gods: "Long ago your ancestors—Terah and his sons Abraham and Nahor—lived beyond the Euphrates and served other gods." Yikes. Hey writer of Genesis, how about throwing us modern readers a bone? What are we supposed to make of Abraham's dallying in idol worship?! And what made his father take his family and just up and leave Ur (no divine command is given to Terah)? Also, what did he do to deserve this special meeting with God and become the father of all Israel?

For some inexplicable reason, these sorts of details are not given. But, if the Abraham tale is another story of Israel in miniature, it begins to make sense. Israel would later also leave Babylon and be led by God into Canaan. Israel's first ancestor came out of Babylon, just as the nation would centuries later. The exile and return to the Promised Land is not entirely a story of Israelite failure: it mirrors the story of their chosen first father. The God who showed himself to be faithful to Abraham will also be faithful to the returnees from exile.

Once we meet Abraham in Genesis 12, the action goes from zero to sixty in just three verses: "Hi Abraham, I'm the God Yahweh. Now follow me to an unknown place so I can make you the father of a new nation and a source of blessing for everyone else." This announcement is a big deal and will follow Israel throughout Genesis and the Old Testament, whether they are in triumph or tragedy: you are blessed and you will be a blessing to all people.

You might notice that these three verses echo God's original creation. Abraham's offspring will be beyond counting, like the stars in the sky or the sand on the shore. Talk about being fruitful and multiplying. We've seen this same use of creation language in the Noah story and we'll see it again later in Genesis. Each stage on Israel's journey is like a "new beginning," a reminder that Israel's story is bound together with the original creation story. This is the flip side of what we saw in chapter 3: the Adam story looks forward to Israel's story; the story of Abraham looks backward to creation.

More Glimpses of Israel's Future

Within a few verses of getting this message from God, Abraham finds himself in the middle of a famine and needing to go down into Egypt to find something to eat. While there, he passes off his wife as his sister to save his own neck (12:10–20). Apparently Sarah is a hot 65-year-old and Abraham is convinced that when the Egyptians get a look at her they will do anything to get her, including killing him. So, he beats them to the punch and simply hands her over. Good move, courageous Abraham, father of a nation. He even gets rich off of the deal.

Later in the story, Abraham sleeps with his wife's servant Hagar to get a son, which he gets, and names him Ishmael. To be fair, this whole "sleep with my servant" idea was actually Sarah's, not Abraham's. Still, Sarah gets jealous and Hagar runs for her life. Hagar comes back, but many years later, Sarah will tell Abraham to get rid of the bastard and his mom. (Did we just flip the channel to daytime TV?) Abraham will agree and send them into the desert with a Dixie Cup full of water. They survive only because of God's intervention.

These episodes highlight how Abraham's story mirrors Israel's. For one thing, even though called by God, Abraham's obedience to God is hardly smooth sailing. In both of these episodes, Abraham's behavior leaves something to be desired, which mimics Israel's struggles with God in a nutshell. If you read the story of Abraham's trip to and from Egypt closely, you'll see it clearly mirrors the exodus story. Abraham enters Egypt because of a famine, as would Joseph and the Israelites at the end of Genesis. Sarah becomes Pharaoh's property, but then he and his household are "plagued" by God for doing so. Pharaoh wants nothing to do with Abraham's God, and summons him to his presence and tells him to leave Egypt, as would another Pharaoh later summon Moses and Aaron and tell the Israelites to leave Egypt. And both Abraham and Israel leave Egypt with a lot of loot.

Perceptive readers of the Bible have noticed the miniature exodus in the Abraham story for a very long time. The Israelites who shaped this story were writing for *their* present time. God has a long track record of delivering his people—even Abraham, the first Israelite—from a foreign land. For these storytellers, Babylonian captivity is not a punishment that threatens Israel's existence as God's people. Rather, it is only one example of a pattern of how God has dealt with the Israelites all along: "Yes, exile was punishment, but it was not the end. Our ancient story says so."

Lots of People and a Land of Their Own

The story of Abraham is fairly long and it covers a lot of ground. But most of the drama focuses on a back-and-forth between God and Abraham about God's promise in Genesis 12 of countless descendants and land. Will Abraham believe God? Will God come through with his promises? It's like watching a sensitive negotiation process, tensions mounting as time ticks away.

As we come to Genesis 15, Abraham expresses some doubt that God will make good on these promises. He tells God, "You have given me no children. I am getting old and can't wait around forever. I am going to take matters into my own hands and make my servant my heir." God volleys back, "You will do no such thing. I will give you a son of your own, as I promised. Not only that, but I will give you a land as well. Just wait."

Abraham believes that God will give him a son (15:6), but he isn't so sure about the land: he wants more proof than just God's word on this one (15:8). So God signs an ancient contract with Abraham. The biblical term is "covenant" and even though we don't use it often in everyday conversation, that's a good word to use for what happens in Genesis 15:8–20. God is making a formal promise to Abraham. He binds himself to come through.

Notice that the covenant in Genesis 15 is all about what God promises to do for Abraham. Other covenants we know from the ancient world between kings and subjects are a two-way street: "I am your king, and here is what I am going to do for you [protection from invaders], and here is what you will do for me [pay me tribute, worship me, don't rebel against me]." God's covenant with Abraham is different: "I am your God and this is what I will do for you." Period. How often do we see an authority figure pledging himself to his subject without at least expecting their vote in November?

God even takes it a step further. In the form of a smoking firepot and blazing torch (God's appearances in the Old Testament are often in the form of fire), he passes in between the severed pieces of sacrificial animals. God was taking an oath: "May I be like these pieces, cut in half, if I don't follow through on the promise." God means business. The plan is going forward no matter what. (Later, in Exodus 2:24–25, we will see that the whole deliverance from Egypt business was all about God keeping this very promise to Abraham.)

Abraham is promised that he will be fruitful and multiply—God will give him a brood of descendants. And he is promised a land for them to call their own, a land that would later be called a land of "milk and honey" (Exodus 3:8), shorthand for a paradise-like piece of property—like Eden. People and land. This promise to Abraham is not random. God is on the move to create a people and place for them in Canaan—

just as God had placed Adam in Eden.

Is Ishmael It?

That's the bird's eye view, but things continue to limp along in the Abraham story. We get to Genesis 16 with Abraham again doubting God's promises of children—or better, acting like God never made any promise at all:

> Now Sarai, Abram's wife, bore him no children. She had an Egyptian slave whose name was Hagar, and Sarai said to Abram, "You see that Yahweh has prevented me from bearing children. Go, sleep with my slave-girl; perhaps I can obtain children by her." And Abram listened to the voice of Sarai.

You have to wonder about this. Is this the way God intends to give Abraham children, though a slave woman rather than his wife? And it doesn't make it any easier that Hagar is Egyptian. Is it through the Egyptians, of all people, that God is going to get things done?

The best spin you can put on this is that Abraham thought Hagar would be the one to bear the children promised to Abraham. After all, Sarah (Sarai for now) was way too old to have children. It's hard to tell if Sarai was just being logical, and Abraham thought, "Yeah, that makes sense." And remember that God didn't mention Sarah in his promise to Abraham; he never said who the mother would be. Also, this type of surrogate mother to ensure descendants is a known practice of the ancient world.

And what does God think of this arrangement? We don't exactly know. He never steps in and says, "How dare you take matters into your own hands like this. You should have waited until I told you what to do!" Could God have been okay with this? Also, Sarah was so mean to Hagar that she ran away into the desert. But God doesn't leave her there. He comes to her rescue—the sort of thing you expect him to do for the Israelites. He tells her to go back to Sarah (who was no doubt happy to see her go). He also promises her that she will have a son and eventually too many descendants to count—which obviously sounds like God's promise to Abraham.

It looks like God is keeping his word to honor Abraham's offspring. Ishmael even gets his own "this is the account" section, although a short one, in Genesis 25:12–18. So, this looks like it is turning out well for Hagar. Yes, but, on the other hand, Ishmael's descendants, the story tells us twice, will be a hostile bunch, picking fights with everyone around them (16:12 and 25:18). This story is pretty involved, but it seems to explain why the Israelites have this long history of tensions with peoples to the south of Canaan and who are also so much like them. As the Israelites tell the story, the sons of Ishmael, these half-brothers, are just born that way. God said so.

So, no, Ishmael is not it. But he comes awfully close. The real son will have old, barren, Sarah as his mother.

Obedient Abraham

Thirteen years pass after the Hagar incident, with no sign of God coming through on the promise. Then, when Abraham is 99 years old, God shows up with a reminder: "Our deal is still on. Land and people still coming your way." But something new is added to the former agreement. Now Abraham has to do something to show his faithfulness to God: circumcise himself and every one of his sons, no exceptions, no end date.

We might not have seen that coming, but Abraham probably did. Circumcision is an ancient ritual practiced by cultures other than just Israel, dating back more than 1,000 years before the time of Abraham. The question, though, is what in the world such a thing signifies. We are not 100 percent sure, and different cultures have different takes on it. Perhaps males were circumcised at puberty as an initiation rite. But Israelite males were circumcised at 8 days old. Some think it was given for hygienic purposes, though that seems a little off topic here in Genesis. Perhaps the organ of procreation was being "claimed" by God to indicate that Abraham's offspring are his.

A simpler explanation is that it was a sign of ethnic identity—"we're in and you're out." Circumcision, whatever the actual cutting symbolizes, is at the very least a physical sign that Abraham has pledged himself to Yahweh. It will be the mark of God's people. Other people the Israelites will encounter (especially the perennial pain-in-the-side Philistines) will be known by the derogatory term "uncircumcised."

We read a bit more about Abraham's side of the agreement in Genesis 18. Three mysterious "visitors" (they seem to be angels and one of them seems to be God) are on their way to nuke Sodom and Gomorrah (that's in chapter 19). They stop and pay a visit to Abraham to tell him that in a year, he and Sarah will have a child. Now the promise of God is getting more specific. But the visitors also relay to Abraham a new piece of information. He needs to "keep the way of the Lord by doing righteousness and justice; so that the Lord may bring about for Abraham what has been promised (18:19)." Up to this point, the promise of a child and land was just that—a promise. But now something is added to the deal. It's like buying a car and being told as you are about to sign, "Oh by the way, there are some taxes and fees we need to discuss."

For this to make any sense, we have to remember who is reading this stuff: Israelites, living in a much later time during their own national crisis. They are in exile because of their failure to follow God's ways. Of course, in Abraham's time there is no formal law of God (that doesn't come until the book of Exodus). So, what is "the way of Yahweh" that is being referred to here? Well, Abraham is being portrayed by later law-abiding Jews as a good law-abiding Jew. It's similar to the way Europeans during the Renaissance would often paint Jesus and Mary to look like very pale Europeans.

We might think of this as "distorting history," but that's our problem. The Israelites saw it as connecting the present with the past, which we have seen all through Genesis so far. We will see Abraham described as a law-keeper again in Genesis 26 when God says to Isaac, "I will make your offspring as numerous as the stars of heaven and will give to your offspring all these lands, and through your offspring all nations on earth will be blessed, because Abraham obeyed my voice and kept my charge, keeping my commands, my statutes and my laws." What are God's "commands, statutes, and laws"? This is classic Old Testament language to refer to the law of Moses, especially Deuteronomy.

These are clearly words intended for later readers, looking back at their own history, to see that their need to follow God's ways is no different than it was in Abraham's day. Israel's ancient history was written for the benefit of a much later audience. This does not mean—just so we are clear—that later Israelites simply made up stories. There is little question that later Israelites were building on ancient stories of their people, perhaps written, perhaps oral. But these stories were given their present shape to help make sense of Israel's identity as a nation in exile.

God Told Abraham to Do What to Isaac?

Throughout Genesis 12–18, we have been going back-and-forth for several decades between Abraham and God, waiting for this promised son to show up. What's taking so long? Why didn't God just get it done right away? Sarah isn't getting any younger, you know. (By the way, in the ancient mindset, whenever a couple is childless, it is the woman's fault. The man is doing his job, so if no child results it must be the woman's problem.) Ishmael was already fourteen years old, and we can imagine the frustration of watching the half-Egyptian slave child grow like a weed while God takes his sweet time coming through.

Of course, the point of all the waiting is to drive home the main point: fulfilling the promise is completely a God thing. This plan of making a new people through Abraham, the new Adam, is wholly God's doing—wholly his creation. Israel exists solely by God's creative act. And we are about to be reminded of that yet another way.

The promised son is finally born in Genesis 21, after decades (or chapters, in our case) of waiting. They name him Isaac, and everyone lives happily ever after. Right? Not in this story. First, Sarah takes the opportunity to do what she wanted to do fourteen years earlier. Now that she had a son of her own, she wants to banish Hagar and Ishmael so that Isaac could claim the entire inheritance for himself without competition. Abraham is a bit upset, but listens to Sarah after God tells him to. Abraham sends them on their way with some food and water, but it soon runs out, and it looks like curtains. But once again, God comes to the rescue, shows her a well, and promises to make Ishmael into a great nation.

We would hope that the birth of a child would make everyone chill just a bit and celebrate, but that doesn't happen. After a good amount of time passes (years, probably), we come to a story that makes you wonder whether Abraham's God isn't a bit arbitrary—even unjust: God tells Abraham to go to Mount Moriah and sacrifice Isaac as a burnt offering.

God is testing Abraham—the story makes this clear in the very first verse (22:1). And, unlike the first Adam, this one is obedient. Abraham makes all the preparations and is about to plunge a knife into his only son, when the angel of Yahweh tells him, at the last second, not to go through with it. The intention is good enough for God. Abraham passed the test.

Great ending. But it's actually a little unnerving to see (1) how willing Abraham is to sacrifice Isaac, and (2) that God couldn't think of a different kind of test. Both of these questions have troubled readers of this story for over 2,000 years. People scramble to try to understand what God is doing—especially since other parts of the Bible say that God hates child sacrifice (e.g., 2 Kings 16:3). And God doesn't appear to be kidding here in Genesis. He couldn't be. For it to be a real test, God had to be serious, and Abraham had to know that God was serious. So God seriously tells Abraham to put Isaac on the chopping block, and there is a real possibility that Abraham is going to go through with it.

Like we said, a lot of people have struggled with this, but we can make some headway by looking at it—and you knew this was coming—from the point of view of later Israelite thinking. The Israelites were against child sacrifice. That's something the pagan gods tell their people to do. But Israel's God still laid some claim on the firstborn. Look at Exodus 13, especially verses 1 and 11–13. The first born of every womb, animal or human, belongs to Yahweh. If the firstborn is an animal, you "give it over" to Yahweh, which means you sacrifice it. A donkey, however, you can "redeem" with a lamb, that is, the lamb can take the place of the donkey (donkeys were unclean animals and were also needed to haul things).

What about firstborn humans? They are redeemed, too. Over in Numbers 8:17, we see another way firstborn humans are redeemed: the tribe of Levi is a stand-in for the firstborn of Israel. God takes that tribe "for himself," not by killing it but by separating it from the other tribes to run the sacrificial system in the tabernacle (and later the Temple). The point is that the Israelite firstborn *still belongs to God.* He just decides not to go through with it and accepts a substitute.

The story of the binding of Isaac makes a bit more sense with that in the background. It is a story about whether God would exercise his right over the firstborn, whether he would actually go through with it and say, "No substitute." Abraham believes that God would not go through with it, as he says in verse 8, that God would replace his son with a lamb—exactly in keeping with Exodus 13 and Numbers 8. With this in mind, the larger point of this story, from a later Israelite point of view, is this: Israel is, was, and always will be God's firstborn son (Exodus 4:22) and is, was, and always will be safe in God's hands—no matter how dire the circumstances.

Genesis will now continue with a few episodes on Isaac, including the death of his mother and father, before moving quickly to Abraham's grandson, Jacob, the true father of the Israelites.

"Rebecca Lights Off the Camel," 18th century Public Domain

9

Genesis 23-25: Isaac Is the Father of Israel

We begin the transition from Abraham to Isaac in Genesis 23 with the death of Sarah at the age of 127. Abraham dies in chapter 25 at the ripe old age of 175. But in between those chapters, Abraham makes his senior household servant swear that he will travel back to his homeland to get a wife for his son rather than pick one from the hated Canaanites, cursed by God since the days of the flood.

The homeland Abraham refers to is not Babylon, but another region in Mesopotamia, Aram-naharaim ("Aram of the two rivers"), in the city of Nahor. This city is not mentioned before, but it looks like it is connected to Abraham's brother Nahor, as we will see in a minute. One of the key ways to make sure your family line remains faithful to Yahweh is not to intermarry with pagan cultures. Throughout the Old Testament, intermarriage is a big no-no for the Israelites (for example, Ezra 9). Intermarriage encourages spiritual infidelity since your love or devotion might lead you to abandon Yahweh and follow the gods of your non-Israelite wife.

So, Abraham made his servant swear he would go back home to find a wife for his son. The servant leaves and finds Isaac a wife rather quickly. Her name is Rebekah, and he finds her by a well. She turns out to be the granddaughter of Abraham's brother Nahor. The servant tells Rebekah's father, Bethuel, and Rebekah's brother, Laban, the story of why he is there. They basically say, "Well, we can't argue with Yahweh, so here you go, take Rebekah." The two of them return to Isaac and it is love at first sight.

At this point, Abraham can die peacefully, knowing his son has married the right kind of woman. After Abraham's death we begin the eighth "this is the account of" section of Genesis, the account of Isaac's family line. In case you are counting though, we have skipped here the seventh account, the account of Ishmael, Abraham's rejected son by Sarah's Egyptian servant, Hagar (Genesis 25:12–18). We mentioned this account in the last chapter, so we don't need to repeat that here—only to say that the main point of this brief genealogy is to underline the hostility between Isaac's descendants, the Israelites, and Ishmael's descendants, the Arabs (which was already hinted at in the little poem of Genesis 16:11–12). But this is just a brief pit stop. The gears shift quickly to the story of Isaac's family.

Isaac Channels Abraham

Note that the "account of Abraham's son Isaac" (25:19) isn't about Isaac at all, but his sons Jacob and Esau—just like the "account of Terah" in 11:27 wasn't about Terah but about his son Abraham. Most of the attention here goes to Jacob, and we will get to him in the next chapter. Isaac, however, plays only a brief, supporting role. The one exception is Genesis 26, when Isaac and Rebekah take a trip to a small town named Gerar. Isaac is driven into a foreign land because of a famine. He goes there to meet with the Philistine king Abimelech to get some help, but when he arrives, he is afraid that the Philistines will kill him and take his smoking hot wife. So he tells Abimelech that Rebekah is really his sister.

Sound familiar? Abraham actually did something similar twice in his day, once in chapter 12 in Egypt (willingly handing over his wife to Pharaoh) and another time, like Isaac, in Gerar (willing to hand over his wife again, this time to another Abimelech, maybe the father or grandfather of Isaac's Abimelech). Isaac's a chip off the old block and God's people just keep running scared to the bad guys for help, don't they?

That's not the only connection to Abraham the writer makes. While in Gerar, God tells Isaac not to follow Abraham's steps to Egypt, but to stay put in Gerar. Gerar is within Israel's future borders. God uses this opportunity to reiterate the promise made originally to Abraham: that he will have land and children. Now that Abraham is dead, the promise is *transferred to Abraham's son.* The promise did not end with Abraham and God isn't finished with his project of creating a new people. The promise is still valid for Abraham's descendants.

The tenacity of God's promise-keeping character will come to a head in the book of Exodus. God delivers the Israelites from Egyptian bondage for one reason: to keep his promise to Abraham (Exodus 2:24–25).

Philistines? Here?

This story also refers to the king of Gerar as Philistine. According to the archaeological record, Philistines weren't living in this region at this time. They didn't make their way from Greece to Canaan until about 1200 B.C. In other words, a reference to the Philistines during the time of Abraham and Isaac is anachronistic. Putting Philistines in this story is like putting a Confederate soldier in *Braveheart*; it just doesn't fit.

We see, once again, that the biblical stories reflect the realities of a later period of time. By the time these stories were written down in the way we have them, the Philistines had been long-time enemies of Israel and occupants of Canaan for centuries. The writer simply took for granted that the Philistines had always been there, which makes perfect sense for a culture that could not consult a library or do a Google search. Or maybe the compilers of the Bible we were well aware that the Philistines were not around in Abraham's time, but they only put them there to "contemporize" the story. This is (more remotely) possible, but the point remains the same: either intentionally or unintentionally, Israel's ancient stories were written for later audiences. Just like we mentioned before, this is another "make Jesus a pale European" moment, a way to connect the Israel of the exile with their ancient past.

This same principle goes for the Hebrew language as well (if you will permit a small but interesting detour). People who study Hebrew for a living (yeah, those people really exist) can tell that the Hebrew language evolved from earlier forms. The Hebrew of the Bible is largely from the time of the kings of Israel, about 800 B.C. and later. So when Genesis tells stories (including Adam and Eve), it does so in a Hebrew that did not exist yet at the time the story is happening.

Once again, this does not mean the stories were made up at this later time. But it does mean that, as the stories were passed down, they were continually transformed to reflect the current time, both in terms of the Hebrew language and actual content. Genesis has ample evidence that this book was written long after the setting for the stories themselves.

Detour over. This story about Isaac handing over his wife is about all we get of him without the stories of Jacob and Esau dominating things. So, just as quickly as we are introduced to Isaac, he is reduced to a supporting role. The story turns to Jacob, or better, the tense relationship between Jacob and his elder brother, Esau.

Benjamin West's "Esau and Jacob Presented to Isaac," 19th century
Public Domain

10

Genesis 25-35: Jacob Is Israel (Literally)

This part of the story of Genesis begins with the birth of not one son but two: Isaac begets Esau and Jacob. As a useful side note, "beget" is just the male version of "birthed." Women "birth" babies, men "beget" them. From their birth we are told that both of these sons are destined to be nations: Jacob's descendants will become Israel and Esau's will be Edom, one of Israel's most notorious enemies.

It doesn't take a lot of insight to see that Jacob will be the focus of the story. But, as it turns out, Jacob is also a liar, and so is his mom Rebekah. There is nothing to be gained from trying to make excuses for either of them. And it's not like Isaac's father and grandfather are models of virtue as they pass off their wives as sisters in order to save their own necks.

Sibling Rivalry

As their descendants will be after them, brothers Jacob and Esau are in conflict with each other. This is not the first time in Genesis brothers had trouble getting along, and it will not be the last. The Cain and Abel story already mirrors the conflict we are about to read about here. A related theme in Genesis and the Old Testament is how the younger brother leapfrogs over the older brother and receives his honor—Moses was the younger brother of Aaron and David was the youngest of a litter of brothers. The younger usurping the older brother is true of Cain. With Abel dead, Cain's other younger brother Seth takes over the place of first importance. We see a similar theme in the story of Jacob and Esau.

Jacob and Esau are fraternal twins that seem destined for conflict from birth: Jacob, the second born, is grasping Esau's heel as he comes out. They grow up and Jacob is presented as a peaceful homebody while Esau is a not-too-bright hairy hunter ("Esau" is Hebrew for hairy). After hunting one day, Esau comes home famished and asks Jacob for some of the red stew he was making. Instead of being a gracious brother or even a normal "bug off, make your own" brother, Jacob uses it as an opportunity to take advantage of his brother's hunger. He reveals his desire to be top dog in the family by striking a deal with Esau: "some stew in exchange for your birthright." Esau agrees, perhaps thinking the agreement means nothing, or that he can get out of it—or perhaps he is just incredibly stupid.

And it seems no one bothers to tell Isaac of the little switcheroo at the stew. I mean, why bother the old man, right? This sets up another confrontation at the end of Isaac's life, when Jacob and Esau are a little older. At this point Isaac is pretty much blind, and apparently a bit senile. He calls for Esau so he can bless him as the firstborn before he dies. Isaac tells Esau to go out, hunt some game, and prepare a tasty meal for him and then he will bless Esau. Instead of replying, "Yeah, um, dad, about that. I sort of sold my birthright to Jacob a while back for some lunch," he goes out, perhaps hoping he can sneak in the blessing without Jacob knowing about it. That is, when he goes out to hunt, he has every intention of breaking the *oath* he *swore* to Jacob.

Rebekah overhears this and thinks fast. Rather than

putting on the brakes and having a family meeting, she tells Jacob what his rat brother is doing. They devise a plan, which does not involve coming clean and telling the truth. Of course not, that would be too easy. Instead, Jacob dresses up like Esau, even down to covering his arms and neck with goatskin (*My, Esau, what hairy and goat-like arms you have!*). Then Rebekah prepares a meal just as Isaac likes it. And the ruse works. They come into Isaac's presence and he asks, "Who is it?" Jacob answers (in his best Esau voice), "I am Esau, your firstborn." Hmm. Isaac is a little skeptical at first. Why does Esau sound like Jacob? But as soon as he gets a whiff of the clothes, all doubts vanish.

Jacob lies to his father to secure the blessing of the firstborn, the birthright he manipulated out of the hands of his oafish brother. Sounds like a job for a family systems therapist with a clear calendar. And have we mentioned that Jacob is the immediate progenitor of the nation of Israel?

Then, like a made-for-TV movie, Esau comes back right after this little ruse, not suspecting a thing. But when he finds out, he is livid for not getting his blessing. And Isaac is livid for having the goatskin pulled over his already blind eyes. Apparently the rules of "trick your father into giving you a blessing" are clear: you can't undo it. The only "blessing" Isaac has left for Esau is no blessing at all: he will live by the sword and serve his brother. That's the best Isaac can do for his firstborn. Sounds more like a curse.

Jacob deceived his father and his brother, even though the birthright was technically his (by nature of the stew deal). Whatever. Esau feels cheated and makes it clear that little brother is a dead man after Isaac dies. So, to protect her boy, Rebekah lies to Isaac again (at least a half lie) by saying that she wants Jacob to go to Haran, where her brother Laban lives, to find a wife—rather than having to choose one of these Hittite women hanging around. Isaac summons Jacob, without mentioning the whole "I am Esau" thing, and tells him to go, and Jacob is only too happy to escape his brother's vengeance. And while Jacob is hiding out from his brother and trying to find a wife, Esau is back home throwing a rebellious pity party. He marries, of all people, a Canaanite woman, thus directly disobeying his father. And can you really blame him?

So Jacob's journey begins. He flees from the anger of his hairy and scary brother and takes refuge with uncle Laban. On the way, he stops for the night at a place that will soon get the name Bethel, which is made up of two Hebrew words meaning "house of God." How did it get that name? That's what this story is designed to tell us. With a stone for a pillow, Jacob falls asleep and has a dream of a ladder going up to heaven with angels going up and down—sort of a portal between heaven and earth. There, at the top, is Yahweh. We might expect God to reprimand Jacob for being a little liar, as any parent would. Instead, he reiterates the promise to Abraham: Jacob's offspring will be uncountable and a blessing to all peoples of the earth.

Biblical scholars typically understand the ladder to heaven story as serving two purposes. One purpose is to stress God's stamp of approval of Jacob, lies and deceits notwithstanding, as the father of the twelve tribes of Israel. Given Israel's less than stellar history later on, an ancestor like Jacob *who still meets with God's approval despite his shortcomings* would be most reassuring. Jacob, like every one of his ancestors, is a flawed hero. Screwing up is deep in Israel's genes; God carrying them along regardless is deeper still. A second purpose is to explain how a prominent city in Israel's later story got its name changed from the older name Luz to "house of God" (in addition to Genesis 29:18, see also Judges 1:23).

Jacob Has Marital Problems, and He Deserves Every Bit of It

Jacob continues his journey and meets his future wife, Rachel, by a well. She is Laban's youngest daughter of two. Jacob is smitten with passion, and Laban promises to let her marry him, but in return for seven years of work. What's seven years hard labor compared to getting to marry your cousin? Jacob gladly agrees, and the time flies. On his wedding night, his bride is brought to his tent for usual wedding night stuff. But in the morning, he is greeted not by Rachel, but by her older (and less attractive) sister, Leah.

Maybe Jacob had too much of the wedding wine—or, perhaps, as poetic justice, he inherited the blindness of his father. It seems that the trickster just got tricked. He should have known Laban was up to no good. It wasn't customary to marry off the younger daughter without getting rid of the older one first. But he didn't see that coming and so now he is stuck with Leah. At any rate, Jacob got a dose of his own medicine. He had earlier used Esau's urges to manipulate him out of his right as firstborn. Driven by his urges, Jacob is now tricked into giving the elder sibling what she deserved. Payback for what he did to Esau. But at least Laban offers him another deal. Jacob can work another seven years and get Rachel too. And he does.

Soon the story focuses on another sibling rivalry: which sister can have more kids for Jacob? Leah is quite fertile while Rachel is barren (as was Sarah). So, Jacob winds up begetting seven children by Leah (six boys, one girl). Rachel gets jealous of all the babies Leah is having and gives her servant Bilhah to Jacob so he can have children through her (again, the echoes with the Abraham and Sarah story are clear). The servant gives him two boys.

At this point, Leah's proverbial well seems to have run dry, so she gives Jacob her servant Zilpah, who gives him two more boys. Then Rachel finally has a son of her own, Joseph, who will become a central figure in a few chapters. Later, she will die giving birth to her second child and another important figure, Benjamin.

What a mess. From the beginning, Jacob's story, with all its shady characters, plays like a reality show. And at the end of it all, we have twelve sons. The nation of Israel is born out of family dysfunction, which will be with them throughout their existence.

More Trickery

By now, Jacob had spent quite enough time with his shady father-in-law/uncle, and he decides to leave. But Laban has experienced the fruits of the promise. He tells Jacob, "You can't go. I know that I am being blessed because of you." Sounds like God is making good on his promise that Abraham's offspring will bring blessing for the nations. So, Jacob agrees to stay and take care of Laban's flocks on one condition: Laban allows Jacob to keep the speckled, spotted, and dark animals. And in a heavy dose of irony, Jacob says, "And you know you can trust me. I am an honest man." Good one, Jacob.

Now it's Laban who falls for a trick, which seems to involve a magical mating ritual of some sort: animals that look at striped branches whenever they are mating will produce striped and spotted babies. Not exactly sure what to do with that, but it sounds like a bit of folklore, like spinning gold from straw. The point, however, is that Jacob once again profits from his deception. When Laban's sons start getting suspicious and Laban gets a bit moody toward Jacob, Jacob does what he does best: he avoids the conflict and takes off for Bethel, which is where God told Jacob to go in the "stairway to heaven" dream.

If it were only that easy. Laban chases after him, but not for the reason we might suspect. Yes, he feels cheated by Jacob (who doesn't at this point?), but Laban's main beef is that his household gods are missing. Apparently, this is a big enough issue to motivate a chase of several hundred miles from Paddan-Aram to Gilead. Laban catches up to Jacob and confronts him about the gods. Jacob, not knowing that Rachel has taken them, tells Jacob that whoever in his camp has the gods "will not live."

We need to pause here and ask: What in the world is Laban doing with household gods, and why in the world would Jacob's wife, of all people, want them around? Weren't Abraham and Isaac both careful to get wives from their family members so that they would be faithful to Yahweh? These people are just a heartbeat away from the father of the twelve tribes and they are still dabbling with other gods! True, the prohibitions against idols and such are not given in the story until Mt. Sinai (in the book of Exodus). We could excuse their behavior as ignorance. But if Israel is shaping its story, as we've seen, why not leave out—or at least massage—the deceit, disbelief, and idolatry? (The author of Chronicles has no problem doing this, for example, when he leaves out David's sin with Bathsheba in his telling of Israel's story.)

The answer, once again, is that the stories in Genesis mirror Israel's later history. The Israelites, from beginning to end, are not models of faithfulness to God and virtue. Yet, how does God react to all this? He does not overlook these misdeeds, as a clueless father might allow his children to run amuck in a restaurant. Rather, he disciplines his people and then presses on with the plan anyway, even with a less than stellar cast of characters. God looks past the inadequacies of his people to execute his plan to bring order back into a chaotic world.

God will always live up to his end of the bargain he made with Abraham—even to a people in exile. And talk about an inadequacy, Jacob, the father of the nation of Israel, married into a family that has "household idols." Mingling with foreign idols is a constant issue with Israel later on, and the ultimate cause for why Israel wound up as the guests of the Babylonians for fifty years or so. That constant struggle is reflected here in the story of Jacob.

God's unwavering faithfulness is summed up in a Hebrew word, *chesed* (CHEH-sed), which can also be understood as love. It's not the kind of love we have for McDonald's chicken nuggets, but what you find in the sixty-year commitment and marriage of Allie and Noah in *The Notebook*. It means that God is sticking to his people no matter what. Again, this is not to condone bad behavior in Israel, but to draw attention to God's character: "This is the kind of God we worship, a God who is compassionate and faithful." You might even say that part of the reason Israel's story is told in this way is to draw attention away from Israel and toward God. That this story would succeed, given the track record of the characters in it, is unlikely, to put it mildly.

Back to Rachel, who stole her father's idols. She is a trickster, a chip off the old block and just like her husband. While Laban was searching for his gods in Leah's tent, she took the gods, put them on her saddle and then sat on them. When he came over to her, she politely said, "I would love to get down and give you a big hug, dad . . . but, unfortunately, it's that time of the month." Crisis averted, and Jacob and Laban agree to be at peace, provided Jacob promises never to mistreat his daughters or to take other wives. With this, Jacob's twenty-year relationship with Laban comes to an end. Jacob arrived there a single man, and he is leaving wealthy and the father of the twelve tribes of Israel. It looks like the fortunes of a people are turning for the better.

A Wrestling Match and a Family Reunion

The inevitable reunion between Jacob and Esau is upon us. Chapter 32 opens with Jacob heading back down into Esau's territory. A messenger sends word that Esau is on his way to meet Jacob, which prompts the obvious, nervous, question: Will this be a reunion or a battle? "Oh," the messenger adds, "did I mention Esau is bringing 400 men with him?" If Jacob was hoping for hugs and kisses, the 400 men with Esau suggest otherwise. The squirmy mama's boy Jacob versus the mighty and hairy hunter plus 400 men? It's not looking good. So Jacob—stop us if you've heard this one—tries to manipulate the situation in his favor. Although, this time he prays to God to save him and then he sends gifts to pacify Esau.

That night, as his gifts are on their way to Esau, Jacob finds himself in what is surely one of the oddest and most seemingly random episodes in Genesis: he has an all-night wrestling match with "a man," or at least that is what we are told at first. Jacob is apparently quite a physical stud, and the man, seeing that he is not able to subdue Jacob, disables him by touching his hip socket. Then he adds, "Let me go, it is almost daybreak."

Is this mysterious figure a vampire, or just tired? This episode is puzzling. A man attacks Jacob at night, can't overpower him, yet is able to knock Jacob's joint out of whack with one touch. No doubt this seems random in the story. But Jacob seems to know this is not just a normal fight. He tells the man he will not let go unless he blesses him. The man agrees and blesses Jacob by changing his name to "Israel," which means, "He struggles with God."

The very name of God's people is a window into things to come. Israel's self-understanding is one of being in a locked battle with God. In their very name, the Israelites make very plain and public that they see themselves as a people that struggle with God. That struggle will take on many dimensions: for example, Job's struggles with God's justice; Qoheleth's struggle with God's unreliability (in Ecclesiastes); many psalmists who wonder out loud "Where is God when you need him?" This is not a people who see themselves as triumphant, tops on the food chain, but as a wandering, wondering people who—to use the vernacular of our day—struggle with their faith.

This "man" becomes less human as Jacob realizes that he has not been engaged in a wrestling match with the neighborhood bully shepherd, but with God himself. And as a reminder of this epic encounter, Jacob hereafter walks with a limp because of his hip injury, which Genesis then describes as the reason why "to this day Israelites do not eat the tendon attached to the socket of the hip."

Like their father before them, the Israelites are defined by the struggle with God. And like Jacob, they intend to hold on to God so they can be blessed. Israel is determined to stay in their struggle with God for as long as it takes. Even exile, however utterly discouraging that may be, will not dissuade them.

Whatever else this story means, in the flow of the narrative, it is used to prepare Jacob for his inevitable meeting with Esau. He has grown up in his struggle with God and now he acts like a man. Before his encounter with God, he is a coward who sends gifts to pacify his angry brother. Now he courageously moves from the back to the front of his entourage and meets his brother face-to-face. And when he gets there, he bows before Esau seven times, a sign of total submission known to us from other ancient cultures. Even today, think about having offended someone, and in a very public gesture, going up to them in a supermarket, street, church, whatever, and bowing to the ground seven times. Utter, self-imposed humiliation. And what does Esau do in response to this gesture? Instead of a knife to the back, he gives Jacob a genuine man hug. The brothers are reunited and Israel is a new man.

After their reunion, Jacob practically begs Esau to accept the "gift" of livestock that was brought to him. The Hebrew word for "gift" here is the same word used earlier for the "blessing" stolen by Jacob at the beginning of the story. So to tie up the loose ends, in a symbolic gesture, Jacob offers back to his brother the blessing that is properly his. That is, out of the blessing he received from God, he now returns that blessing to his brother. And notice how Esau reacts. Not "gimmie, gimmie." Rather, he only accepts because Jacob is insistent.

These two brothers have come a long way. The very thing they quarreled over and that caused so much family dissension is now something they want the other to have in a most desperate way. Perhaps Israel is starting to behave like Israel should. The seed of the promise to Abraham is beginning to sprout. God has blessed Israel and through him others are being blessed.

Now an independent and rich man with nothing to fear from his brother, Israel goes on to settle near the city of Shechem, which is in Canaan. Abraham had also passed through there (12:6). Israel buys a parcel of land, digs a well (a way of laying claim to the land), and builds an altar that he names *El Elohe Yisrael* [ale eh-lo-HEY yis-rah-ALE], which means something like "mighty is the God of Israel." Israel is beginning to take hold of Canaan, the land of promise. As we will see throughout Israel's story, the Canaanites didn't exactly hold a "welcome to the neighborhood" party. They weren't excited about Yahweh moving in next door.

At the end of Israel's life, he moves from Shechem and returns to Paddan-Aram where his name was changed. All is well. The command to increase their number is repeated: God's promise of people and land are still a go. The story ends with a list of Israel's twelve sons and the deaths of Rachel, then Isaac. And the last sentence ends on a hopeful note of reconciliation: Isaac is buried by both sons, Israel and Esau (35:29). It seems we are poised to move onto the last phase of the story of Genesis.

Pontormo's "Joseph in Egypt," 16th century Public Domain

11

Genesis 36-50: Israel Is Saved

We have come a long way in Genesis—from Adam to Seth to Noah to Abraham, Isaac, and Jacob. This is the main line of descent the writer is tracing out. But along the way we have also met the rejected sons: Cain, Ishmael, and Esau. The writer doesn't want us to forget about them. He even used up one of his "this is the account of" sections to make sure we didn't forget about Ishmael (25:12–18), a seven-verse reminder before we move on to the story of Jacob and Esau. Genesis 36 is similar, the ninth "this is the account of" section, an entire chapter dedicated to the descendants of Esau before we move on to the next episode in the main story.

We have seen throughout Genesis how the story reflects a later time—as late as the exile to Babylon and the return. As we saw back in chapter one of this book, the list of Edomite kings in Genesis 36:31–40 is another example. The list is introduced in verse 31: "These are the kings who reigned in the land of Edom, before any king reigned over the Israelites." This statement makes no sense unless the writer lived in a time when Israel's kings were currently ruling or had ruled at some point in the past. This would have been no earlier than about 1000 B.C., if not later, in exilic times.

Genesis is a story that looks back, over the centuries, to talk about the days of old. We might be beating a dead horse, but getting on board with this is central to reading Genesis through ancient eyes, that is, through the eyes of those who wrote the story as we have it today.

Genesis 37 brings us to the tenth and final "this is the account of" section divider in Genesis, this one dedicated to the line of Jacob through his favorite son, Joseph, firstborn of his favorite wife, Rachel. Joseph will play a vital role in the survival of his people. And we may know it as one of the better-known stories in the Bible, if only because of the famous "Amazing Technicolor Dreamcoat," inspirer of children's coloring books and Broadway musicals alike. But this story is really about what happens to the line of Jacob (now named Israel). Genesis is the story of the beginning of Israel.

An Annoying Younger Brother Lands on His Feet

Joseph, like most every other character we've encountered so far, starts off with some pretty serious character flaws, but turns out to be key figure in God's plan. At the outset, Joseph is a bootlicking daddy's boy. Israel even gave Joseph this beautiful robe, which he no doubt wore around his brothers, flaunting his favored status. The 17-year-old even tattles on his brothers.

We hope the Genesis theme of sibling rivalry is ringing loud and true in your ears at this point—Cain and Abel, Jacob and Esau, now Joseph and his brothers. What gives? Israel's national history will be one big sibling rivalry event. The twelve brothers will in time become the twelve tribes of Israel, who will—wait for it—not get along. At all. The kingdom of Israel, unified under David and Solomon, will quickly split into two kingdoms, ten tribes making up the north and the remaining two (Judah and Benjamin) making up the south. Sibling rivalry is a civil war in miniature.

So, Joseph's brothers hate him—not just because of the snappy clothes, but because Joseph rubs it in their faces. Joseph has two dreams with the same message: he will one day rule over his brothers. Having the dreams is one thing, but Joseph makes sure his brothers know about them. Do you think they are going to welcome this news with open arms? We didn't think so. It's eleven angry brothers against one cocky and spoiled teenager.

One day, they see him coming from a distance and say, "Here comes that dreamer . . . let's kill him." But, after some debate, cooler heads prevail and they take his robe and throw him into a well. When a caravan of Ishmaelite (Arabic) traders passes by on the way to Egypt, the brothers sell Joseph to them. They get some quick cash and they get rid of the problem. It's a win-win. To cover up their crime, they dip the coveted robe in goat's blood and then tell their father that his favorite son has been ripped apart by wild animals. Here we go again—yet another incident with brothers that involves blood (think Abel) and deception (think Jacob). And again, Jacob, the great deceiver, gets another dose of his own medicine: he falls for the ruse.

Jacob is devastated. His favorite son from his favorite wife is dead. Little does he know that Joseph is making his way to Egypt to be sold as a slave to Potiphar, one of Pharaoh's high-ranking officials. Joseph quickly becomes a trusted man in Potiphar's court. He is put in charge of Potiphar's house and we see the promise to Abraham at work again: God blesses Potiphar because Potiphar "blessed" Joseph (39:5). Potiphar trusts him completely.

Too bad Joseph is a total stud and Potiphar's wife has a thing for him. One day, while they are alone in the house, she tries to seduce him, but Joseph refuses. Unfortunately, she has a good hold of his tunic, and so when Joseph tries to get out of there, he has to go without his clothes. This is the second time in this story he lost his clothing (remember the Technicolor robe), with tragic results. Immediately, the scorned and guilty woman lies to the household servants and to Potiphar, telling them that it was Joseph who tried to seduce her. Who is Potiphar going to believe? He throws Joseph in jail, just like his brothers had thrown him in the pit. The guy can't catch a break.

Or can he? We already learned that Joseph has coded dreams. In those days, the ability to interpret dreams was a valuable art. And it just so happens that while Joseph is in prison, Pharaoh's cupbearer and baker, already incarcerated, each have a dream that they simply can't make heads or tails of. Joseph interprets the cupbearer's dream: he would be released from prison and restored to Pharaoh's good graces. Joseph then interprets the baker's dream, which is less promising: he would have his head chopped off and stuck on a pole for bird food.

Both dreams come true and Joseph asks the cupbearer to put in a good word for him with Pharaoh. And in line with Joseph's bad luck, the cupbearer forgets. That is, until Pharaoh starts having some dreams of his own that need interpreting.

Joseph's Dream Comes True

Since we live in a world of the never-ending *Saw* movies and Freddie Kruger, we might not be that creeped out by dreams of skinny cows eating fat cows, or—if you can picture it—skinny stalks of wheat eating fat stalks of wheat. But for Pharaoh these dreams are disturbing. His own magicians cannot not tell him what the dreams mean, and that is their job. So, the cupbearer says, "Hey, I remember. I was in prison with this Hebrew guy who is quite good at interpreting dreams." Pharaoh calls for Joseph. "I hear you can interpret dreams," says Pharaoh. "Actually," Joseph replies, "God interprets dreams, Pharaoh. I am just the messenger" (which tells you Joseph may have learned some humility while staring at his prison walls).

So, Pharaoh relays his dreams (nightmares, really) to

Joseph about scrawny cows/wheat eating fat cows/wheat, and Joseph immediately knows what they mean: Egypt will have seven years of abundance (fat cows/wheat) followed by seven years of famine (scrawny cows/wheat), and the famine will be much worse than the abundant years. So, Pharaoh takes a chance and asks the prisoner Joseph what he thinks they should do about it. Joseph says to store up food during the seven years of abundance so they will have enough to ration out during the years of famine. Good call, Joseph.

So Joseph, a Hebrew prisoner, saves Egypt from destruction. Several generations later, these same Egyptians would turn on the Hebrews and enslave them. Bad form, Egypt. But that's a story for another book.

While Joseph is promoted from slave to Pharaoh's right hand man in charge of preparing for the famine, Jacob and his growing family are still back in the land of Canaan. The famine hits and Jacob starts to feel the pinch. He sends his remaining sons (except for Benjamin, the only other son of his favorite wife, Rachel) to Egypt to see if they can buy some grain from Pharaoh.

And please tell us you've seen this "go to Egypt because of a famine" idea before. This episode here, which sets up the end of Genesis that leads to Israel's enslavement in Egypt, mirrors Abraham's trek to Egypt back in Genesis 12. And just like that earlier story where Sarah is a "guest" in Pharaoh's house, Joseph's brothers will soon find themselves in an awkward situation in Pharaoh's house. That same scene comes home to roost big-time in the book of Exodus—where this story is headed—when the Israelites are slaves to Pharaoh.

Joseph's brothers come to Egypt and, wouldn't you know it, they must meet with Joseph, who is now the one in charge of rationing the food. He recognizes them immediately, but they don't recognize him. Instead, they bow down to him in fulfillment of the dream he had as a boy. The story could have come to a quick end here, but the writer has more to say. Payback is not the point. There is a deeper lesson his readers need to learn.

God Delivers Israel

The brothers are completely vulnerable, but instead of revealing who he is, Joseph plays a little trick on them. He accuses them of spying. He strikes a deal: "Show me you are honest men by bringing back this youngest brother of yours you say you have." They are less than excited about this deal, since they know Jacob will not want to risk it. He's a little gun-shy with his favorite remaining child after the Joseph ordeal. But, having no real choice, they leave another brother, Simeon, as collateral. He is bound in chains and the remaining brothers make their way back to Canaan with a heavy message to deliver.

The brothers deserve every bit of this. They have to deliver another piece of bad news to their father about another one of Rachel's sons. Only, this time it is the truth. They must have been pondering this bit of poetic justice on the long journey home.

Jacob refuses, and we can't blame him. Joseph is lost and Simeon is as good as lost. He will not lose another son. The thing is, though, that the famine does not subside, and they soon run out of the grain they bought on the first trip. So rather than lose all of his family to the famine, Jacob relents out of desperation and sends the sons back with a lot of gifts in the hopes of making sure he gets his Benjamin back. They stay for a while in Egypt and are treated very well. And Benjamin, far from being in harm's way, is given five times as much to eat and drink as anyone else.

But it's all a set-up. Joseph isn't going to let them off that easily. The brothers leave, greatly relieved, with all the grain they can carry. What they don't know is that trickster Joseph had planted his silver cup in Benjamin's bag and is about to accuse them of stealing it. Joseph's men ride after them, catch up with them, and promptly arrest them for stealing the cup. The brothers plead innocence, but it is announced that the one who has the cup will be returned to Egypt as a slave. Joseph is re-enacting his own story with the other favorite son while his brothers helplessly watch. After the cup is found they all return to Joseph to beg for his mercy. To return without Benjamin might literally kill their aging father.

Fortunately for his brothers, Joseph feels he has punished them enough. His heart is breaking and he reveals his identity to his brothers, who simply can't believe what they are seeing. And, in a statement of not only forgiveness but spiritual maturity, he tell his brothers that this was God's plan all along: "God sent me before you to preserve for you a remnant on earth, and to keep alive for you many survivors. So, it was not you who sent me here, but God; he has made me a father to Pharaoh, and lord of all his house and ruler over all the land of Egypt" (45:7–8).

Change a few words and the Israelites could be saying the same thing after the Exodus and especially the return from Babylonian exile—"God preserved us, a remnant, and delivered us from harm." If you do a word search for "remnant" in Ezra, Isaiah, and Jeremiah, you can see how closely that idea is tied to Israel's return from exile. With great joy, Joseph sends his brothers back and Pharaoh himself invites Joseph's entire family to join him in Egypt. He even gives them the land of Goshen, the best of the land, on the outskirts of Egypt.

The brothers arrive back in Canaan and give Jacob the news. He is stunned and overjoyed. All of the people of Israel migrate to Egypt and this is where they remain as we end the story of Genesis. And they do quite well for themselves. They prosper, and, more importantly, they "were fruitful and increased greatly in number" (47:27). After all we have seen of these Israelites—one misstep after another—God is still with them blessing them and increasing their number, in keeping with the ancient command of creation.

As Genesis comes to a close, we see Jacob growing very old and near death. And, in his last act as patriarch, he blesses each of his sons beginning with Joseph's two sons, Ephraim and Manasseh. He insists, though, on blessing Ephraim the younger over Manasseh the elder. Here we go again: the preference of the younger over the older. Joseph's blessings make it clear that a special place will be given to Ephraim and Judah, a glimpse of

Israel's future. Ephraim will be the center of the northern kingdom and Judah will be the center of the southern kingdom. In fact, Ephraim and Judah will become shorthand for the northern and southern kingdoms, respectively. Judah receives an especially exalted place in Jacob's blessing, for all Israel's hopes will be pinned on a king from Judah. His name will be David.

The book ends with the death of Jacob and then Joseph. With this, Israel's infancy comes to an end and a difficult period of growth is about to begin. The movement from a people to a nation is not one that will come easily—it will end with Israel licking its wounds from Babylonian captivity. And as we have seen, that larger story is already in view throughout Genesis. Israel's ancient story is one of struggle, with God and with others. It is also a story of Israel's faith in God, that he will come through for them no matter what. Genesis is Israel's story to show that God can be counted on, from the very beginning.

Conclusion: Now What?

The book of Genesis just sort of stops cold, doesn't it? No nice conclusion to wrap things up. If you are feeling that Genesis just leaves you hanging, you're not wrong. You're picking up on the role Genesis plays in the story of Israel—it's just the beginning. It's not meant to draw loose ends together and give you a resolution. It's meant to tease you into reading how the story of this large (and getting larger by the minute) family will pan out as they continue the struggle with God, with highs and lows, peaks and valleys. That story will eventually find Israel in exile in Babylon, that great national tragedy that fuels their vision for writing their grand story, what we call the Old Testament.

We know we didn't cover everything. We warned you about that at the beginning. There are some episodes we only glanced at and others we just couldn't get to at all. We kept our focus on helping you to look at Genesis as an *ancient story.* That means trying, as best as we can, to lay aside what we as modern Christians *think* Genesis is saying or *ought* to be saying and pay closer attention to what the *ancient* author was actually saying to his *ancient* readers. In this book, we helped put you on the right road, pointed you in the right direction, and gave you a big push.

Happy travels.

We also didn't get into some of those sexy issues that drive people to have endless Facebook debates—things like evolution, the Big Bang theory, and whether dinosaurs were on the ark. To be honest, we hope that as you learn to read Genesis as an ancient story you will discover that Genesis isn't set up to answer those sorts of questions. Genesis was written to answer ancient questions for ancient Israelites. Whatever you think Genesis *means* for us today, you need to start by understanding what Genesis *meant* back then.

It's up to you to now to (1) go back and read Genesis, filling out some of the details we weren't able to cover and discovering the ancient story for yourself, and (2) keep going, reading the story in Exodus and beyond, always with ancient eyes. If you are interested in learning more about reading Genesis with ancient eyes, we have included some reading suggestions that go into a little more detail. But—again—even these are only scratching the surface. Reading Genesis and all of Scripture is a lifelong process of learning, adjustment, and refinement.

Welcome to the journey.

Guide for Group Discussions

It has come to our attention that some of our readers are reading *Genesis for Normal People* in groups. So, we thought it would be helpful for you to have some type of guide for group discussions. We especially thought this would be of help to group leaders as they prepare and guide these groups.

So, here it is.

For each chapter we have written:

- *Summary*: a brief recap of each chapter.
- *Discussion Questions*: prompts to help spark conversation. (Some questions are rather open-ended, while others require you to do some digging in the biblical text.)
- *Notes for Leaders*: A brief note is added to some questions to help leaders prepare and also lead the group in conversation. (We also recommend a good study Bible to help fill in more information where needed.)

1. The Genesis of Genesis

Summary

Genesis is not a textbook or personal moral guide. Genesis is a story and should be read like one. It creates a different world for us and then invites us in, leaving aside our world, as all great stories do. This perspective does not say whether or not Genesis is historically accurate; it simply informs us on how we should approach the book and what we can expect from it.

Genesis is also an *ancient* story. As such, it must be read with ancient eyes so we can ask questions it is prepared to answer. Genesis was most likely composed in its present form just after Israel's exile in Babylon in the 6th century B.C. Given this context, we should read remembering that Genesis is part of Israel's story written in response to Israel's national catastrophe to encourage continued faithfulness to God.

Finally, Genesis is also part of a larger story. This means it can't be read in isolation but as part of something bigger. Just like you wouldn't read the first Harry Potter book and think you are done, Genesis is part of a five-book series called the Pentateuch or Torah. The message of the Pentateuch is that God is worthy of Israel's worship because he is (1) the creator and (2) the savior of Israel. Genesis focuses on (1) but hints throughout at (2).

Discussion Questions with Notes for Leaders

1. Would you say you grew up reading the Bible as a textbook, instruction guide, or a story? What are some benefits and dangers to each of these?

2. How does reading Genesis as the first book in a five-part series differ from reading it as a stand-alone book? What changes?

3. Does accepting that Moses didn't write Genesis affect any of your other beliefs? Why or why not? (*Note for Leaders: Many believe it is important to maintain that Moses is the author of the Pentateuch. The reasoning is that Moses would be an eyewitness to the events, which would make the Pentateuch, therefore, historically reliable. What is or is not at stake here?*)

2. Genesis from 30,000 Feet

Summary

Genesis takes us from creation to the doorstep of Israel's slavery in Egypt, which will be picked up in the next book, Exodus. Genesis tells this story by dividing the book, not into chapters and verse numbers, but into ten sections that begin "This is this is the account of [so and so]." This arrangement reminds us that Genesis is telling the beginning of *Israel's* story.

Genesis is not about the world as a whole, even if it includes a creation story. It is a story about Israel's relationship with God that is marked by struggle (which is what "Israel" means) over the twin issues of people and land.

Discussion Questions with Notes for Leaders

1. As Christians, we believe that Genesis is a story about Israel *by* Israelites, but we also believe that the Bible is God's Word to us today. How do both of these statements relate to each other? What does it mean for how you read your Bible as God's Word? (*Note for leaders: Some feel that for the Bible to be God's Word for us, it can't be too locked in to the ancient context. Or, perhaps, they feel that we need to rise above the ancient context to find a general principle (moral) of the story. Talking about what it means to read passages "in context" might be a good introduction for a discussion.)*

2. We mentioned that originally the Bible didn't have chapters or verses. In what ways do you think that might affect how you read your Bible? *(Note for leaders: One effect would be that you really have to know the story well in order to locate a passage in a numberless Bible. You would have to be able to glance at a sentence or two and know where you are in the story.)*

3. Genesis 1: Yahweh Is Better

Summary

The story of creation in Genesis 1 is an ancient story written by and for ancient Israelites. For us to understand it, we must learn to read it through ancient eyes, suspending our twenty-first-century views of science. "In the beginning" there was already a watery chaos (the deep) that covered everything and that made life impossible.

The watery state made the cosmos a "formless void" (*tohubohu*). Genesis 1 tells how God gave "form" to the cosmos in Days 1–3, and then filled the emptiness in Days 3–6. The story of creation in Genesis 1 is not about "creation out of nothing," but God ordering chaos and then filling that ordered space with the heavenly bodies (Day 4), sea creatures and birds (Day 5), and land creatures and, finally, humans (Day 6).

Rather than presenting a scientific account of creation, Genesis 1 plays off of themes shared by other, older, ancient cultures, especially Babylonian cultures (for example, stories like *Enuma Elish*). But the author of this story does not just repeat these themes. Instead, he transforms and subverts them to make the case that Israel's God, not the gods of the other nations, is the true chaos tamer.

If Genesis 1 is read with modern expectations instead of ancient eyes, the meaning of this story will be obscured. To respect and more fully understand the story, we must read it as it was meant to be read.

Discussion Questions with Notes for Leaders

1. Read 2 Peter 3:5 in light of Genesis 1. Does your view of God change if he is presented as the One who orders chaos rather than the One who creates out of nothing? How? Why? (*Note for Leaders: One thought is that God is ready and willing to allow himself to be talked about in the*

Bible in a manner that reflects the cultural mindset in which the Bible was written.)

2. Do you think the Bible and science are fundamentally at odds, or are they in harmony? Why?

3. The word Genesis 1 uses for humans being created in God's "image" is also found in Ezekiel 7:20, 16:17, and 23:14. Based on those verses and the brief mention of kingly representatives in the book, discuss what Genesis means by the notion that humans are created in God's image. How is that the same or different than what you previously thought? (*Note for Leaders: Often people think of the image of God as our ability to reason, use language, or commune with God. But what do these passages say about what "image" means?)*

4. Genesis 2–4: Adam Is Israel

Summary

The story of Adam and Eve is neither a continuation of Genesis 1 nor another version of the creation of the cosmos. It is a different kind of story altogether. It shifts the focus of Genesis from the cosmos to Israel. Genesis 1 sets up the big picture of what kind of God Israel worships; Genesis 2–4 is a preview of Israel's long journey in the Old Testament as a whole.

We can see in the story of Adam's son Cain that there are clearly other people outside of the Garden of Eden populating the earth. So, Adam is not the first human. Rather, the Adam story is a story of Israel in miniature, a preview of coming attractions. The stories of Adam and Israel parallel each other. Both Adam and Israel are God's special people, placed in a lush land (Adam in Eden, Israel in Canaan), and given "law" to obey (Adam is commanded not to eat of the Tree of the Knowledge of

Good and Evil, and Israel is given the Law of Moses).

Staying in the land is contingent upon obedience. Adam and Eve disobey and are exiled from the Garden; Israel disobeys and is exiled from the Promised Land. For both Adam and Israel, exile is a form of death (which helps explain God's promise in Genesis 2:17 that Adam will die "on the day" he eats of the fruit, but his actual punishment in Genesis 3:23–24 is to be driven from the Garden).

The Adam story is also similar to the book of Proverbs. As Israel is called to seek wisdom by walking along God's path and living according to his wisdom, Adam and Eve are being taught to gain wisdom by obeying God (don't eat the fruit of the tree of knowledge) and trusting God. In both cases, living in wise submission to God's ways brings with it the promise of life, which means primarily life in the land (Eden or Canaan). Adam and Eve's failure to live the wise life is a miniature version of Israel's repeated failures to do likewise.

Discussion Questions with Notes for Leaders

1. Read Romans 5:12–20. Discuss how this passage from Paul affects reading the story of Adam as a miniature Israel. (*Note for Leaders: Paul seems to assume that Adam is the first man [not a preview of Israel as a nation] who brought on a universal problem that Jesus came to solve.)*

2. How does recognizing that people were living *outside* the Garden of Eden while the story of Adam and Eve is happening *inside* the Garden of Eden affect your view of human origins? (*Note for Leaders: Some think that if Adam is not the first man, much of the tension with evolution diminishes.)*

3. We mentioned that, in the Western church at least, the story of the eating of the forbidden fruit has been told to explain original sin and the Fall. The Eastern church, on the other hand, has recounted the story as a loss of

innocence. What interpretation resonates most with you? Why?

5. Genesis 4–5: Cain Is a Fool

Summary

The first sin committed in the Bible is Cain killing Abel, his younger brother, out of jealousy. In doing so, Cain is following in his father Adam's footsteps in not obeying God's direction. And, like the Adam story, this is also a story of Israel in miniature. In Proverbs 1, the failure to follow the path of wisdom results in a murder, which mirrors Cain's behavior.

Adam, Eve, and Cain were already in exile outside of the Garden, but Cain's act leads him further away. He wanders in the land of Nod ("wandering"), where he starts a new life. Meanwhile, Adam and Eve have another son, Seth, who has a son named Enosh. Instead of building him a city as Cain does for his son (Enoch), the birth of Enosh marks the time when "people began to call on the name of Yahweh" (4:26). The line of Seth eventually leads to Abraham, the father of Israel.

The genealogy of the fifth chapter moves the story forward to the next major episode, the flood. The genealogy is like a map, making sure we know that the story is headed down Seth's line leading to Noah. The superhuman lifespans are not to be taken literally. They indicate that death came much more slowly before the flood.

Discussion Questions with Notes for Leaders

1. Read Proverbs 1. What connections do you see with Cain's story in Genesis 4? How do you explain these connections? What do you think this means for how the Bible came together? (*Note for Leaders: Too often, the notion of wisdom is seen as a secondary issue in the Bible*

behind the "more important" narratives of Genesis through 2 Kings. Perhaps wisdom plays a more prominent role throughout the Bible than we expect. A good introduction to your conversation is to discuss: "What is biblical wisdom?")

2. Based just on the story of Adam and Eve and then the story of Cain and Abel, discuss sin. What is it and where did it come from?

3. We mention the "Sumerian King List," an ancient document from one of Israel's neighbors that says kings lived thousands of years. Do you think the ages in Genesis 5 are meant to be actual life spans or to make a statement about life before the flood? Why? (*Note for Leaders: This is another example of an issue that is relevant throughout Genesis: how historically accurate is Genesis, and how important is historical accuracy for how we think of the Bible and inspiration?)*

6. Genesis 6–9: Everyone Is Annihilated

Summary

The story of the flood is not a children's story but a horrific account of the mass extinction of humanity. Israel's neighbors also had flood stories very similar to and older than the biblical one. The best-known examples are found in the epics of *Gilgamesh* and *Atrahasis*. The likely background for all of these flood stories is a devastating deluge in the Mesopotamian plain around 2900 B.C.

The flood stories were written to given an account of why such a thing happened, and the reason had to do with something happening in the divine realm. The Israelites told their own version of the flood story to point out how their God is different from the gods of the other nations. The flood was not punishment for humans making too much noise (as in *Atrahasis*), but for failing to follow God's ways that lead to life (not to mention the incident in Genesis 6:1–4, where divine beings cohabited with women).

Most importantly, the flood story depicts the reversal of creation—the undoing of the order God had established in Genesis 1. The windows of the dome above the earth that kept the upper waters at bay (Day 2, Genesis 1:6–8) were opened, and the waters of chaos came crashing back down, killing everything. The cosmos, in other words, returned to its original, formless, and uninhabitable (*tohubohu*) state.

The flood story ends with an incident involving Noah's three sons. Ham is singled out as guilty of finding his father drunk and naked and then telling his brothers about it. The punishment for this act is a curse on Ham's son, Canaan, one of Israel's archenemies in the Old Testament. The flood story is a vehicle for the later Israelite writer to explain why the hated Canaanites deserved everything they got, including being exterminated from their homeland so it could be given to the Israelites.

Discussion Questions with Notes for Leaders

1. What implications are there to reading the flood as universal rather than regional?

2. What are the major themes of the flood story as you read it? Is it helpful or unhelpful to teach children this story at a young age? Why or why not?

3. As you are introduced to stories like *Atrahasis* and the *Gilgamesh*, what are your reactions to these other stories and their similarities to stories in Genesis?

4. The flood story is designed to talk about *why* God would destroy people with natural disasters. What do you think

is the relationship between natural disasters and God today? Is it the same or different than the relationship we see in the Bible? Why? (*Note for Leaders: Some think that "natural" disasters happen apart from God, while God is responsible only for special acts [miracles]. Others think that God is ultimately behind what we call "natural" events, not because God causes storms or directly causes the sun to rise every day, but because God is the one who ordered creation to do these things.)*

7. Genesis 10–11: Babylon Is Evil

Summary

Chapter 10 is a post-flood genealogy of Noah's three sons: Shem, Ham, and Japheth. The descendants of each settle in different parts of the known world with their own language. The line of Shem (Shem is the word from which we get "Semitic") leads to Abraham, who dominates the next fourteen chapters. But first, we come to the famous story of the tower of Babel.

Like the story of creation and the flood, the tower story is another jab at the Babylonians, the nation that destroyed the temple and took the Israelites into captivity in 586 B.C. They are the ones responsible for the confusion of languages on the earth (an alternate explanation for the rise of languages than the genealogy above). They were also foolish enough to think they could build a tower (actually, a stepped structure called a ziggurat) to reach to the level of the gods. Instead, God *comes down* and punishes them by confusing (the Hebrew for "confusing" is *balal*, a pun on *babel*, that is, Babylon) their language and scattering them. The point of the story is that the Babylonians have been an annoying, destructive, and godless force since the beginning.

Discussion Questions with Notes for Leaders

1. How would you explain how there are "many languages" in Genesis 10 and "one language" in Genesis 11? What do you think is the author's point in putting those two stories back-to-back?

2. According to the tower of Babel story, God comes down while the Babylonians are attempting to reach up to the gods. As we think of the Bible as a whole, and especially Jesus in the New Testament, what implications are there for having a God who comes down? (*Note for Leaders: It seems God meets us where we are, which is an expression of love and grace.)*

3. According to Joshua 24:2, Terah, Abraham's father, worshipped other gods in Babylon. The text is silent, but do you think Abraham would have gone along with that? Does this affect your view of Abraham? Why or why not? (*Note for Leaders: Jewish interpreters especially have tried to keep Abraham distant from any hint that he was an idol worshipper. Note, also, that Abraham was not called until after the family arrived in Haran, but Genesis 15:7 says that God called Abraham out of Ur.)*

8. Genesis 12–22: Abraham Is Chosen

Summary

God chooses Abraham, a former resident of Babylon, to become the father of a nation (Israel) and a source of blessing or curse on all the other nations (depending on how they act toward Israel). No reason is given for why Abraham was chosen. However, Abraham coming out of Babylon to enter the land of Canaan and make it his home mirrors Israel coming out of

Babylon and returning to her homeland after the exile.

Abraham is not a saint, which is another similarity between him and Israel. He mimics Israel's struggles with God in a nutshell, as when he tries (twice) to save his own neck by passing off Sarah as a sister. The first incident takes place in Genesis 12 when Abraham and Sarah go down into Egypt because of a famine and then return to Canaan, which mirrors Israel's journey to and from Egypt later.

The drama that underscores the Abraham story is Sarah's barrenness. God promises to provide offspring for Abraham through Sarah and to give his descendants the land of Canaan as their home. At first, it looked as if the promise would have to be fulfilled through Abraham's servant Eliezer or through Ishmael, the son of Sarah's Egyptian maidservant, Hagar. But, as if to make the point that Israel's existence is wholly God's doing, the promise would be fulfilled through Isaac, the son of the barren woman.

The story of Abraham also introduces us to the rite of circumcision, which would be a physical sign of Israel's binding covenant with Yahweh. That is the part of the bargain that Abraham and his descendants will have to keep. Another obligation is hinted at in 18:19, where Abraham is to "keep the way of the Lord by doing righteousness and justice" in order to remain in good standing with Yahweh. Maintaining a clear Israelite identity by keeping God's law was a core concern of the Israelites who were in exile in Babylon, and the Abraham story reflects that concern.

After all of these promises, God tells Abraham to sacrifice his son Isaac (now a teenager), which is a test to see whether Abraham is fully obedient to God (unlike Adam). The angel of Yahweh stops Abraham at the last minute. As harsh as this story is to our ears, it is rooted in the biblical notion that the firstborn of every womb—human or animal—belongs to Yahweh.

Discussion Questions with Notes for Leaders

1. For lack of space, this book doesn't address the account of

Sodom and Gomorrah in Genesis 18–19. Read the story. Based on what you've learned about how to read Genesis, what do you think is the point of the story? Why do you think this episode is put in Genesis at this point of the story? (*Note for Leaders: This episode does not fit seamlessly into the story, but look at how Abraham's behavior contrasts with that of Lot in chapter 13 and also the people of Sodom in chapter 19. Another key issue here is the announcement of Sarah's eventual pregnancy.)*

2. What is the point of God asking Abraham to sacrifice Isaac? Why do you think God does this? (*Note for Leaders: The story clearly states that this is a test so God can know [find out] whether Abraham trusts him. Throughout much of Genesis, God is portrayed in very human-like terms [anthropomorphically]. Also, throughout church history, theologians have seen the near-sacrifice of Isaac as a foreshadowing of Christ.)*

3. God's promise to Abraham seems to be unconditional before Genesis 17 (God will give him land and offspring). But beginning in chapter 17, the promises take on some conditions (like circumcision and the sacrifice of Isaac). How does one reconcile this?

9. Genesis 23–25: Isaac Is the Father of Israel

Summary

Abraham arranges for Isaac to find a wife from Aram-naharaim, a region on Mesopotamia with family connections to Abraham. Intermarriage was generally a bad idea in the Old Testament because it encouraged spiritual infidelity. So, Isaac marries Rebekah, granddaughter of Abraham's brother, Nahor. Rebekah's brother is Laban, whom we will meet again later on in the story of Jacob.

With the death of Abraham, the promises of God are transferred to Isaac. Like his father before him, Isaac wanders into the foreign land (because of a famine) of Gerar, which is in the land of the Philistines. God delivers him and his wife safe and sound. The promise of land and offspring do not come to an end with Abraham's death.

The presence of Philistines in the early second millennium B.C. is out of place historically, since they only made their way to Canaan from Greece around 1200 B.C. This is simply another indication that Israel's story of ancient times was written later than the setting of the stories.

Discussion Questions with Notes for Leaders

1. Abraham and Isaac (in chapter 26) both tell kings that their wives are their sisters. Does this raise any moral issues? Why do you think the author of Genesis includes all of these accounts? (*Note for Leaders: Technically, Sarah was Abraham's half-sister and Rebekah was Isaac's sort-of sister [cousin], but the men's motives seem self-serving: personal survival.)*

2. All of Genesis 23 details the death and burial of Sarah, though we didn't really cover it in the book. Why do you think the author of Genesis spends so much time on this account? (*Note for Leaders: By buying a burial plot, Abraham now has some legal claim on the land that will eventually be given to the Israelites after the Exodus.)*

3. Reread the story of Cain and Abel in Genesis 4. How is the account of the birth of Jacob and Esau (Genesis 25:19–34) similar, and how is it different?

10. Genesis 25–35: Jacob Is Israel (Literally)

Summary

Jacob and his fraternal twin Esau are the two sons of Isaac and Rebekah. The sibling rivalry is front and center, as it was in the story of Cain and Abel. This will be a common theme throughout Israel's tribal and national existence. (The twelve tribes of Israel are descended from Jacob's twelve sons, and we see regular fighting and tension between them.)

The story of Jacob and Esau is fraught with deception, namely on the part of Jacob and his mother against Esau and Isaac. The issue is which of the brothers would have the right of the firstborn, the elder Esau (who sold his birthright for a warm lunch) or Jacob (who connived with his mother to fool blind Isaac into blessing him over Esau). This arrangement sparks a lot of hostility, and Jacob winds up fleeing for safety. Along the way, he has a dream at Bethel ("house of God") where he sees a ladder going to heaven, and God's promise of land and children is transferred to him.

Jacob continues on his journey and meets Rachel, the daughter of his uncle Laban, and more trickery is afoot. He agrees to work for Laban for seven years in exchange for Rachel, but Laban tricks him by replacing her with Leah, Rachel's less attractive but older sister—poetic justice for Jacob usurping Esau's rightful place as firstborn. Jacob is outsmarted, but Laban offers him Rachel as well, in exchange for seven more years. This touches off a sibling rivalry between the sisters as with Jacob and Esau. From these two sisters and their two servants, Jacob has twelve sons, who will become the twelve tribes of Israel.

After a while, Jacob wants to move away with his family, but not before tricking Laban into giving him an awful lot of speckled, spotted, and dark animals. Laban tolerates it until he notices his household gods are missing. At that point, he chases Jacob down to confront him about the gods. Jacob has no idea what is going on, but he promises that whoever took them is as good as dead. Unfortunately, the culprit is Rachel, but she tricks Laban (lies to him) in order to be let go. Despite Israel's early track record of deceitful behavior, God sticks with them—as he will in bringing them back from exile in Babylon.

Jacob continues on his journey through Esau's territory and is understandably nervous. He sends gifts to appease his brother, and during the night engages in a wrestling match with "a man" who blesses him and changes his name to "Israel" ("he struggles with God")—a name that will describe Israel's existence throughout her upcoming history. Like their father before them, the Israelites are defined by their struggle with God to be blessed. Even the ultimate struggle of exile will not dissuade them.

Discussion Questions with Notes for Leaders

1. How does the family dysfunction of Israel's story in Genesis affect the way you see God's relationship to Israel—and perhaps yourself?

2. One of the major themes of Genesis is struggling or wrestling with God. There is a longstanding tradition of wrestling with God in the Jewish tradition, but Christians are often discouraged from wrestling with God. Were you raised in a tradition where "wrestling with God" was allowed? What do you think are appropriate and inappropriate ways to relate to God? Think of other biblical examples of people who struggled. (*Note for Leaders: Many biblical characters struggled with God, such as Moses, David, Job, and Qohelet [the main figure in Ecclesiastes, sometimes referred to as the "teacher"]. About half of the psalms have a strong element of lament, and Jesus himself wrestled with God.)*

3. Jacob has some highly questionable character flaws. What are some of these flaws? God doesn't seem to address these flaws. How does this affect your view of "God as

God," as presented in Genesis? (*Note for Leaders: This is a good place to talk about the theme of trickery we have seen throughout Genesis.)*

11. Genesis 36–50: Israel Is Saved

Summary

This final section of Genesis focuses on the line of Jacob through his favorite son, Joseph. It takes us from a squabbling brood of brothers to the doorsteps of Pharaoh's kingdom. Although the story in Genesis ends well, it is prelude to Israel's enslavement of the Israelites in the book of Exodus.

Sibling rivalry, a theme we have seen throughout Genesis, is a central issue in these chapters. Joseph is his father's favorite, and he tried to hold it over his brothers. It doesn't help that Joseph has dreams, which he relays to his brothers, that they will one day bow to him. They sell Joseph to traders and eventually Joseph ends up in Egypt. Discord will continue throughout Israel's history with the twelve tribes of Israel who are descended from these twelve brothers.

Another familiar theme we see in this story is trickery. Jacob's sons fool him into believing that a wild animal killed Joseph. The irony we see is the same we saw with Laban earlier: Jacob, the trickster, is tricked. Later, Joseph will conceal his identity from his brothers and fool them into thinking their lives are in danger for stealing a cup.

Joseph's presence in Egypt brings blessing to Egypt, and he and his family are blessed by Egypt. Through Joseph's interpretation of Pharaoh's dreams, Egypt is spared a deadly famine and Joseph's family is taken from the brink of starvation into the safety of Pharaoh's kingdom. Such mutual benefit is an outworking of God's promise to Abraham (Genesis 12:1–3)—that his descendants will be a blessing to other nations and they in turn will be blessed by the nations.

While in Egypt, the children of Jacob "were fruitful and increased greatly in number" (Genesis 47:27). These words are first seen in Genesis 1 (and at other pivotal moments in the book), and so our story has come full-circle. Israel, God's chosen people, has gone from a barren couple to a large clan and is growing into a nation at the heart of one of the political superpowers of the day.

The book ends with the death of Jacob, then Joseph. With this, Israel's infancy comes to an end and a difficult period of growth is about to begin. The movement from a people to a nation is not one that will come easily. It will end with Israel licking its wounds from Babylonian captivity. Israel's ancient story—in Genesis and the entire Old Testament—is one of struggle with God and with others. It is also a story of Israel's persistent faith in God and belief that he will come through for them no matter what.

Discussion Questions with Notes for Leaders

1. Because of space, our book doesn't address the account of Judah and Tamar in Genesis 38. Read the story. Based on what you've learned about how to read Genesis, talk about the point of the story and why you think this episode is put in Genesis at this point of the story. (*Note for Leaders: Like the story of Sodom and Gomorrah, the story of Judah and Tamar seems like an interruption in the flow of Genesis. Some think it is inserted here mainly to build suspense, but it also invites a contrast between Joseph's honorable actions toward Potiphar's wife and Judah's dishonorable sexual relations with his own daughter-in-law. The child of their union, Perez, would be the ancestor of King David.*)
2. In Genesis 42–44, Joseph seemingly treats his brothers poorly, stringing them along in their desperate position. Why does he do this? Is he vindictive, or are there other possible reasons why the author of Genesis would include this portrayal of Joseph?

3. Joseph makes his mark because of his ability to interpret dreams by God's hand. Do you think dreams are a way that God speaks to us?
4. How does the story of Joseph set up the book of Exodus? (*Note for Leaders: The opening verses of Exodus are very similar to Genesis 46:26–27, which reminds us that Exodus is not a separate book, but the next chapter in a larger story. Also, the inhospitality shown to Israel by Pharaoh in the first chapter of Exodus contrasts with their royal treatment in the Joseph story, and also paints Egypt in a very bad light. Like the residents of Sodom, Egypt will later show disrespect to their guests.*)

Further Reading

Brueggemann, Walter. *Genesis*. Atlanta, GA: John Knox Press, 1982.

Enns, Peter. *Invitation to Genesis*. Nashville, TN: Abingdon Press, 2006.

Enns, Peter. *The Evolution of Adam: What the Bible Does and Doesn't Say About Human Origins*. Grand Rapids, MI: Brazos Press, 2012.

Goldingay, John. *Genesis for Everyone: Parts 1 and 2*. Louisville, KY: Westminster John Knox Press, 2010.

Longman III, Tremper. *How to Read Genesis*. Downers Grove, IL: InterVarsity Press, 2005.

Middleton, J. Richard. *The Liberating Image: The Imago Dei in Genesis 1*. Grand Rapids, MI: Brazos Press, 2005.

Sacks, Jonathan. *Covenant & Conversation, Genesis: The Book of Beginnings*. London: Maggid Books, 2009.

Sarna, Nahum. *Understanding Genesis: The World of the Bible in the Light of History*. New York, NY: Schocken Books, 1970.

Walton, John. *The Lost World of Genesis One: Ancient Cosmology and the Origins Debate*. Downers Grove, IL: InterVarsity Press, 2009.

About the Authors

Peter Enns (Ph.D., Harvard University) teaches Biblical Studies at Eastern University in St. Davids, Pennsylvania. He has also taught courses at several institutions, including Princeton Theological Seminary, Fuller Theological Seminary, and Westminster Theological Seminary. His books include *Inspiration and Incarnation: Evangelicals and the Problem of the Old Testament* and *The Evolution of Adam: What the Bible Does and Doesn't Say about Human Origins*. Peter blogs at http://www.patheos.com/blogs/peterenns/. He and his wife live in Lansdale, Pennsylvania and have three grown children.

Jared Byas, M.A., teaches courses in both ethics and the Old Testament at Grand Canyon University in Phoenix, Arizona. He spent several years as a teaching pastor in the Philadelphia area and currently writes on Christianity and culture in various publications, including http://jbyas.com. He lives in Phoenix with his wife and three kids.

CPSIA information can be obtained
at www.ICGtesting.com
Printed in the USA
BVOW10s1955230717
489702BV00007B/84/P